H . H . Richardson

In this book leading scholars reconsider the significance of the late nineteenth-century American architect Henry Hobson Richardson, perhaps best known for his design of Boston's Trinity Church. Against the long-held view of Richardson as an isolated and proto-modernist genius, they argue for a broader understanding of his work within the context of his times. Viewed this way, Richardson becomes a more challenging figure—an architect who in many ways was shaped by and was consistent with his era, even as he dominated it. In addition to shedding new light on the architect, the book shows how much Richardson scholarship has changed and matured over the course of a century.

Maureen Meister is Associate Professor of Art History at the Art Institute of Boston.

"In an age given to debunking, Richardson's reputation has never seemed greater. These spirited and eloquent essays by the scholars who know him best remind us why he remains a central figure in America's intellectual and cultural history."
MICHAEL J. LEWIS, Williams College, author of *The Politics of the German Gothic Revival*

"This anthology provides close readings of important H. H. Richardson buildings, primarily in North Easton, by the leading scholars of his work. The essays explore the maturity of Richardson's production, provide richer contexts for these structures, and assess a unique matrix of patrons, designer, and place."
KEITH N. MORGAN, Professor of Art History, Boston University

H . H . Richardson

The Architect,

His Peers, AND

Their Era. edited by

MAUREEN

MEISTER

The MIT Press

Cambridge, Massachusetts • London, England

Published in cooperation with the Oakes Ames Memorial Hall Association, North Easton, Massachusetts

This book was set in Garamond 3.
Printed and bound in the United States of America.

Library of Congress Cataloging-in-Publication Data
H. H. Richardson : the architect, his peers, and their era / edited by
  Maureen Meister.
       p.   cm.
    Includes bibliographical references and index.
    ISBN 0-262-13356-3 (hc : alk. paper)
    1. Richardson, H. H. (Henry Hobson), 1838–1886—Criticism
and interpretation.   I. Meister, Maureen.
NA737.R5H2   1999
720´.92—dc21   99-26903
                                                            CIP

In memoriam

Margaret Henderson Floyd

1932–1997

· CONTENTS ·

ILLUSTRATIONS

Maureen Meister

During the past few months, while preparing this collection of essays for publication, I have been thinking about who our readers might be. On one hand, I have recognized that these essays will be read critically by scholars. On the other hand, I have hoped that the essays will find readers among enthusiasts, including the residents of Easton, Massachusetts, where a colloquium on H. H. Richardson was held in September of 1996 at Oakes Ames Memorial Hall, designed by Richardson and built between 1879 and 1881. At the colloquium, earlier versions of the papers in this volume were presented.

Yet a third group of readers has been of interest to me— the students, sitting at library tables and carrels, probably doing research for papers on topics relating to Richardson. This book, then, has been shaped to take its place beside the books by Mariana Griswold Van Rensselaer, Henry-Russell Hitchcock, James F. O'Gorman, Jeffrey Karl Ochsner, and Margaret Henderson Floyd. In those books, the reader will find overviews of Richardson's architectural career.

By contrast, this volume offers more focused insights. Through a close examination of Oakes Ames Memorial Hall, Thomas C. Hubka considers the influence of the English critic and author John Ruskin on Richardson's design method.

Margaret Floyd also focuses on a single building: the Robert Treat Paine house in Waltham, Massachusetts. She explores the context of Richardson's era, identifying a variety of interests that were shared by Boston architects, and she explains how these interests manifest themselves in the Paine house. Francis R. Kowsky examines the influence of the landscape architect Frederick Law Olmsted on Richardson. James O'Gorman also considers the relationship between Richardson and an architect of his era, Frank Furness, though O'Gorman seeks to clarify our understanding by presenting a comparison rather than by examining the influence of one architect on another. Finally, Jeffrey Ochsner studies the nature of the architecture that Richardson inspired during the 1880s and early 1890s, called Richardsonian Romanesque.

Throughout these essays, a common theme is the authors' desire to question a view of Richardson's buildings promoted from the 1930s on by Hitchcock and others. That view presented Richardson as a kind of proto-modernist while ignoring the picturesque, Victorian qualities of his work. Today's Richardson scholars are more accepting of these qualities. In their other academic work, they are reconsidering Richardson's era and the many lesser-known architects of his generation. In these essays, the reader will encounter explicit analyses of the changing nature of the scholarly study of Richardson and his career.

Our contributors' varying research interests have been essential to their interpretation of Richardson's work. O'Gorman, who has written extensively on Richardson, has also written extensively on Furness. In 1998 he published *Accomplished in All Departments of Art: Hammatt Billings of*

Boston, 1818–1874, presenting a study of a lesser-known yet once-prominent Boston architect. The late Margaret Henderson Floyd was an authority on many lesser-known Boston architects, most notably John Hubbard Sturgis. She was author of a book on architectural education in Boston and another book on the firm of Longfellow, Alden and Harlow.

In 1998 Kowsky published *Country, Park, and City: The Architecture and Life of Calvert Vaux.* Vaux, who worked during the nineteenth century in New York City as both an architect and landscape architect, was for a time Olmsted's partner. Kowsky's interest in landscape design and his broader concern with nineteenth-century ideas about nature are pursued in his essay.

Both Hubka and Ochsner are architects and teach architecture students. Hubka's interest in Richardson's design process grows out of his professional orientation. He is completing a book on Eastern European synagogues of the eighteenth century, a topic that may seem far removed from Richardson. As forms, however, these timbered structures with fantastic roof systems are linked to Hubka's interest in the picturesque aspects of Richardson's work.

Ochsner's interest in Richardson began more than twenty years ago, when from his family's home in Rhode Island he visited Richardson's buildings. His catalog of Richardson's buildings, published in 1982, grew from his search for more information after those visits. Although he has continued to research and publish on Richardson, his recent work has focused on Pacific Northwest architecture, including buildings that reflect Richardson's influence.

When the Richardson colloquium was held at Memorial Hall in 1996, it was moderated by William H. Pierson, Jr., and he introduces this book. Pierson is a founding co-editor of the Buildings of the United States, a series of books published by the Society of Architectural Historians. He also is author of the first two volumes of *American Buildings and Their Architects* and currently is writing the third volume, *The Architecture of Abundance*, which focuses on the late nineteenth century.

With the documentation of Richardson's buildings and his life established, if never fully complete, and with the publication by O'Gorman and Floyd of two fine monographs with excellent color photographs, Richardson scholars are widening their vision. In this collection, the authors place Richardson in a broader context, making Richardson a more challenging figure: an architect who, in many ways, was shaped by his era and was consistent with it, even as he dominated it.

Acknowledgments

It is my pleasure and privilege to thank the many people who have made the publication of this book possible.

All of the essay contributors helped out in a variety of ways, beyond submitting their manuscripts and photographs. I want to express my appreciation to them for their efforts, including their generous advice. In particular, I'd like to single out Jeffrey Ochsner for being especially helpful on a number of occasions. Also I'd like to thank William Floyd for his responsiveness to my requests, which came at a tragic time in his life. In the months before and after his wife Margaret's death, Bill answered my calls and shared Margaret's files with me so that her paper would be published.

This publication also received assistance from George Hersey, Yale University; Richard Chafee, Providence, R.I.; and Sarah Bradford Landau, New York University.

My husband, David Feigenbaum, deserves recognition as well. He unfailingly and patiently responded to my requests for computer-related services: he scanned and converted and retrieved and more.

I also want to thank the people who worked on this book for the MIT Press; they have made this publication experience an entirely positive one. Roger L. Conover, Julie Grimaldi, and Matthew Abbate shepherded the volume through its various phases, from acquisition to production. Alice Falk, copy editor, and Jean Wilcox, graphic designer, contributed significantly, making the book theirs as well.

A source of essential funding for the publication of this book was a grant from the Graham Foundation for Advanced Studies in the Fine Arts. Generous financial support has also come from Frederick L. Ames, who has been devoted to this volume in many ways. Respectful of his family's legacy, he conceived and organized the H. H. Richardson colloquium in North Easton, Massachusetts, held in 1996. From the start, he recognized that the contributors' work should be preserved through publication.

And finally, I would like to acknowledge the assistance that was given by Margaret Henderson Floyd to the colloquium and the book. Fred Ames has often commented on Margaret's role in helping him identify participants and in developing a strategy for publishing the essays. With her typical enthusiasm, Margaret willingly wrote letters and made phone calls. All of us who were involved in this project knew Margaret and have been helped by her at one time or another in the past. We were deeply saddened by her death in 1997. Unable to offer thanks, we dedicate this volume to her memory.

THE BEAUTY OF A BELIEF:
The Ames Family, Richardson, and Unitarianism

William H. Pierson, Jr.

The buildings of North Easton, Massachusetts, tell a very special American story: a story about the dynamic relationship between an industrious and benevolent American family and America's most thoroughly national asset, its rich and abundant land. The first phase of this relationship began in 1803, when Oliver Ames purchased water rights and a scattering of industrial buildings on the Queset River in what is now North Easton and began manufacturing the most basic of all land tools, the shovel. His timing could not have been better. Not only was the newly born nation aggressively on the move, shaping and reshaping itself in its search for national identity, but at almost the same moment that Oliver Ames set the waterwheels of his new enterprise in motion, Thomas Jefferson negotiated the Louisiana Purchase. This brilliant strategic move added almost nine hundred thousand square miles of virgin land to the nation's holdings, doubling its size; and Jefferson wasted no time in assessing the new land's potential. Even before the deal with France was closed, he had organized the Lewis and Clark expedition, and by the fall of 1803 it was on its way to explore this vast new acquisition. "Old Oliver," as he was called, may have had no idea of what these events portended for his future business, but there can be no question that Meriwether Lewis and William Clark opened the eyes of America to both the wonders and the riches of the West and triggered the western migration that by midcentury became a flood. Together with the demands of the rapidly developing nation, this dynamic movement created an ever-growing market for shovels, and the O. Ames Company was running smoothly and fully alert to the opportunities that were opening to it.

Oliver Ames's shovel manufactory was a success from the beginning, not only because he was in the right place at the right time but also because of his ingenious and efficient management of the operation: he made his shovels lighter than the British shovels, which then dominated the American market, and he quickened the production process by relying on water power wherever possible. For the first quarter century, he managed the company alone; but in the 1820s two of his sons, Oakes and Oliver, Jr., joined the firm as laborers. They worked their way up through the company until 1844, when Old Oliver retired and turned the management over to them. By then, Ames shovels were being marketed nationwide. Indeed, at the fundamental level of the earth itself, the company became a primary force in the shaping of the American land.

The rapid expansion of the nation that favored the Ames Company also created a challenging problem. Both the distance and remoteness of many of their new markets made delivery of their shovels increasingly difficult. When the two brothers took over the company, long-distance freight was carried primarily by water—by sea between major seaports, by navigable rivers and other waterways inland—and then by animal haulage to its final destination. These were all slow and plodding means. In the early 1830s, however, the steam-powered railroad made its appearance in the United States, and Oliver Ames was even then supplying shovels for construction. By midcentury more than three thousand miles of track had been laid. One of those early efforts was the Boston and Providence line, which passed less than ten miles west of North Easton, and Oakes and Oliver, Jr., saw at once the possibilities: in 1855 they created the Easton Branch Railroad, a spur line that connected North Easton with the larger system. This gave the Ames family an active and productive role in the development of the railroad, the scope of which established them as leading openers as well as shapers of the land. Drawn irresistibly to the West by its dazzling promise, and eager to share in its abundant offerings, they invested heavily in the Union Pacific Railway, which was then building westward from Nebraska. Oliver, Jr., was actually president of that company for five years (1866–1871), and during that time, largely through his efforts, 667 miles of new westward track were laid. In 1869, at Ogden, Utah, they met the tracks of the Central Pacific building eastward from California, and the famous golden spike was driven to form the first transcontinental line in the United States. It was a dramatic climax to one of the most daring engineering feats of the century, and the Ames brothers were directly involved.

While all this was going on, the town of North Easton was growing steadily in response to the success of the Ames Company. It was, after all, a company town. As in most early industrial communities in New England, however, growth was random, not planned: the shape of both the town and its buildings was determined by the necessities of the manufacturing process and by the practical, social, and spiritual needs of the workers. As each new requirement or development was identified, an existing building was modified or added to, or a new building was built to accommodate its needs. The emphasis was on utility. All buildings, industrial and domestic alike, were conceived in simple conventional terms. They were also solidly built and advantageously located, with respect both to the individual function of each building and to its role in the life of the community as a whole. The result was a dynamic coherence, rooted in a common scale and a common style and brought alive by the natural and human energies that drove the community toward a common end.

Just half a century after Old Oliver came to North Easton, a building appeared in its midst that set the stage for a dramatic change in its stark utilitarian character. By then the third generation of the Ames family was active in the company, and in 1854, the first son of Oakes Ames, Oakes Angier Ames, built himself a Gothic villa. In contrast to the simple rectangular boxes of the existing village, it had a high frontal gable ornamented with a delicate bargeboard. It also had pointed arch and hooded windows and a broad frontal veranda carried on flat Tudor arches sprung from slender Gothic piers. Its walls were a warm variegated local granite laid in rock-faced random ashlar. Located on a modest tract of land on the Queset River, just across the main street and upstream from the shovel shops, it added a brilliant new note to the sober tonality of the existing town.

The design of the house, including the use of rock-faced masonry, was taken directly from the most original and influential house pattern book of the period: Andrew Jackson Downing's *Cottage Residences,* published in 1850. At that time, Downing's was a powerful voice in the shaping of American domestic architecture; and by turning to him for his design, Oakes Angier Ames identified himself with the most advanced notions in American romantic taste. In a manner characteristic of the period, he even gave the house a name derived from its river setting: he called it "Queset." Seen against the prim simplicity of the original village, Queset was a sparkling jewel, and it set a standard of architectural quality that would have momentous consequences for North Easton.

Five years later, Frederick Lothrop Ames, Oakes Angier's cousin, built a more imposing house that introduced into the village a suburban tone more formal than the open picturesque cast of Queset. The house was also situated on a far more spacious piece of land. The site was, in fact, a rising slope in the midst of several acres on the eastern fringes of the town. Here, in contrast to Queset, the mansion stood quite apart from the beat and bustle of the working community. But there was yet another and equally important difference: the house was designed by an architect. That architect was George Snell, who was British-born and London-trained. Thus, when he settled in Boston in 1850, he brought with him the most advanced European ideas about urban house design. F. L. Ames's house was in the Second Empire style of France, a style that originated in Paris, was modulated in London, and first appeared in the United States in the late 1850s. During the following decades, it became a fashionable mode for American civic and urban domestic architecture. The house was among the first of many designed by Snell in that mode and therefore stood on the threshold of a major episode in American domestic architecture; and in a manner appropriate to its high-style character, it had a formal name. Not to be outdone by his cousin, F. L. Ames also derived the name from the natural setting: he called it "Langwater," a dialectal reflection of the long pond that shaped the western border of his property.

Queset and Langwater opened a wholly new dimension in the relationship between members of the Ames family and the American land. Along with their practical roles as shapers and openers, they now became managers and enhancers. This began in their attitude toward the town itself. As their long-standing emphasis on utility became less dominant, they began to see its buildings as capable of fulfilling far more than simple practical needs. They recognized that in the larger circles of life, buildings could also touch the mind and the heart and could make life richer as well as easier. In other words, they began to discover architecture at its most expressive level. This was inevitable. The third generation found themselves in control of a substantial fortune that took them into ever-widening financial interests and brought them into intimate associations with the world beyond the shovel shops. Social and cultural aspirations became motivating forces in their lives.

The dominant figure in this phase of their engagement was Frederick Lothrop Ames. The only son of Oliver II, Frederick was the first of the shovel family to enjoy a college education: after studying at Phillips Exeter Academy, he went on to Harvard, where he graduated at age eighteen in 1854. He later became one of the most powerful figures in industrial and financial affairs not only in Boston but in the nation at large. Along with his central role as treasurer of the Ames Company, he was an official of railroads and banks and the largest holder of real estate in Boston. In addition, he was an overseer of Harvard, a mark of distinction that reveals another fascinating side of this truly remarkable man. While a student at Harvard, he found himself in the presence of some of the great minds of his time; especially impressive were the geologist Louis Agassiz and the botanist Asa Gray, who stood at the head of a new and electrifying world of ideas that he would never have experienced in the pragmatic ambience of the shovel shops. Although his public persona remained that of the tough successful financier, privately he was a reflective intellectual with interests that drew him away from North Easton toward the intelligentsia of Boston and Cambridge. Inspired originally by the studies of Asa Gray, he developed a searching interest in horticulture, an enthusiasm that took him ever more deeply into the provocative new ideas and attitudes toward the earth that were challenging conventional concepts; for much of his adult life, he was a prominent figure in the affairs of the Massachusetts Horticultural Society. His passion also forged lifelong friendships, not only with Asa Gray himself but especially with fellow Harvard graduate Charles Sprague Sargent, the dendrologist who was a protégé of Gray's and who in 1873 became the first director of Harvard's Arnold

Arboretum. Ames played an active role in the Arboretum project, to which he was also a major contributor.

Sargent lived near the Arboretum in the wealthy suburb of Brookline, where his 150-acre family estate, Holm Lea, was a showpiece of nineteenth-century landscape gardening. F. L. Ames was a familiar and welcome figure at Holm Lea as well as the Arboretum, and it was surely in this context that he first came together with the other two principal players in the transformation of North Easton, the architect Henry Hobson Richardson and the landscape architect Frederick Law Olmsted. Richardson moved to Brookline in 1874, to a rented house directly across the road from Sargent's Holm Lea. He came to the area from New York to supervise the construction of his first major commission, Trinity Church in Boston. With his impeccable family credentials, his Harvard education, his social grace, and his creative powers, the architect quickly and easily took his place in this high-energy community of prominent achievers. More than that, the fact that Richardson's family firm in New Orleans, the Priestly and Bien Hardware Company, was an outlet for Ames shovels in the deep South makes it almost certain that F. L. Ames and Richardson at the very least knew about one another. It could not have been long after the architect's arrival in Brookline that the two came together and began the intimate and productive friendship that would culminate in one of the most remarkable architectural achievements of nineteenth-century America.

The third partner in that achievement, Frederick Law Olmsted, entered the picture in the summer of 1878 when he began working on the preliminary plans for the Arnold Arboretum as part of the Boston Park System. Because of his work at Central Park in New York City, Olmsted was already recognized as the leading figure in the field of landscape planning and was surely known to F. L. Ames by reputation. Beyond that, their mutual involvement in the Arboretum project made it inevitable that they would meet personally and begin the association that would bring Olmsted, along with Richardson, to North Easton.

The North Easton enterprise began on 9 March 1877 when F. L. Ames's father, Oliver II, died and left $50,000 to construct a free library for the town. The motivation for this enlightened gift, dedicated as it was to the intellectual life of the entire community, can be traced to the Unitarian roots of the Ames family. Unitarianism was a major spiritual and intellectual force in New England during the late nineteenth century. To appreciate its impact on places such as North Easton, we must briefly examine Unitarianism more generally, especially as it was practiced in the United States. The most conspicuous tenet of the movement was its rejection of the Trinity in favor of a single God; and in New England the image of that God was tempered by the pervasive presence of transcendentalism. In this, the Unitarians stripped away the dogma and mysticism of Christianity, thus humanizing it and making it more relevant to the everyday conduct of life. At the same time, they were also in open revolt against the inhibiting doctrine of the orthodox Congregational Church. Rejecting the harsh Calvinist image of an angry God of reprobation standing in judgment over depraved man, the Unitarians believed in a nurturing God of love; they also believed that man was created in the image of that God and was thus perfectible in his capacity to love. Although they adhered to the Bible as the primary source of religious truth, they also sought truth wherever it was to be found through the exercise of free will. They respected the individual and in their relationships with one another expected kindness, tolerance, and above all love; to them, fellowship with one another was as important in nurturing those ideals as the worship service itself.

From the very beginning, North Easton was in some measure shaped and directed by Unitarianism. Even though the workforce held diverse and largely conventional religious beliefs, the Ames family itself was ardently Unitarian, and the active nature of their commitment directly affected both the quality of life and the physical character of the town. Old Oliver was the founder of the Unitarian Society there, and his management of the shovel shops and the town was guided by Unitarian principles: it was disciplined, tolerant, and fair. Following him, his sons were equally motivated. Oliver II not only built a church and a parsonage for the Society, but—displaying unusual tolerance—he also donated a church to the Methodists and together with his brother Oakes gave the land on which the Catholic church was built; by willing a library to the town, he was acting in the most liberal spirit of his Unitarian faith, which taught him to seek and perpetuate truth.

No one in the Ames family understood this better than Frederick Lothrop Ames. The sturdy Unitarian convictions instilled in him by his heritage were broadened and deepened by his four years at Harvard, which was then the intellectual seat of the Unitarian movement. In carrying out his father's gift, he saw at once the need to match its special nature with a powerful and expressive architectural statement, and there was no question in his mind as to the architect who could best meet that challenge. The commission was given directly to

Richardson without competition. The reasons for this are obvious. On 9 February 1877, exactly one month before Oliver II's death, Richardson's Trinity Church in Boston was dedicated, drawing public acclaim for his triumph and firmly establishing his preeminence among American architects. At the same time, Richardson was even then at work on the Winn Memorial Library in Woburn, north of Boston, the first of his famous small-town libraries. There was thus no question about his qualifications.

But there was also a strong personal bond between the two men. The friendship that so enriched their lives was firmly established by 1877, and Richardson, because of his own powerful Unitarian heritage, would have been more sensitive than any other architect of his time to what F. L. Ames and his family were striving to achieve. Richardson was their man.

With his mind made up about the architect, F. L. Ames wasted no time in carrying out his father's wishes. Richardson received the commission for the library in September 1877, just six months after Oliver II's death. The site was the crest of a gentle slope on the west side of Main Street, in the center of town. To the northwest, where the land dropped off more steeply, it abutted the property of Queset. The two buildings were therefore visually connected. Although essentially contoured by the natural fall of the land, the site was groomed with neat lawns and terraces to accommodate the building, which sat solidly in place. Lines between foundation and ground were thus precisely drawn. In the building itself, the robust random ashlar of its rock-faced granite walls, together with the powerful rhythms of its arched openings and strip windows, brought the picturesque elements introduced into the town by neighboring Queset to new levels of vigor and largeness. Put in musical terms, the fundamental theme of the "architectural symphony" then gathering in North Easton, so gently stated in Queset by the cellos, was developed and monumentalized in the library by the commanding voice of the trombones.

The second of the five buildings that Richardson designed in North Easton was the Oakes Ames Memorial Hall. It was commissioned early in 1879 by the three sons of Oakes Ames, including Oakes Angier Ames, the creator of Queset, who was in charge of the project. It has been called the Town Hall, and it was indeed a gift to the town, but its intended function was not administrative. Rather, like the library, it was a reflection of the Ames family's Unitarian convictions: where the library spoke to their search for truth, the hall addressed their belief in fellowship. On the first floor was a small auditorium and two lesser rooms that, as Jeffrey Ochsner suggests, were almost certainly intended as a dining room and kitchen. The second floor was given over to a large auditorium with a stage spacious enough to accommodate town meetings, lectures, and other forms of public discussion, as well as modest musical events. The third floor was the Masonic Lodge.

The Ames Memorial Hall was situated on a high granite outcropping south of the library, at a point on Main Street where the road split, one branch curving slowly from its southerly course to the east and the other slightly more sharply to the west, where it fed into Lincoln Street. This created a triangle of public land above which the building towered, clearly visible from either direction on Main Street as the hub of the town. To realize the potential of this dynamic location, however, it was necessary to broaden the planning beyond the individual buildings and embrace both the natural and the designed environment. In a decision that would become a defining factor in the developing enhancement of North Easton, Frederick Law Olmsted was invited to do just that. In fact, Richardson sought Olmsted's advice even before the latter became directly associated with the project. Olmsted's active participation was as inevitable as that of Richardson, and for the same reasons: as well as his friendship and professional collaboration with the architect, Olmsted had already come to know F. L. Ames through their mutual involvement with the Arnold Arboretum. Indeed, by this time all three men were key figures in a creative circle of prominent intellectuals and shared many of the same ideals and aspirations. That they should work together at North Easton was not only logical—it was essential, even preordained: and the results had meaning as subtle and profound as the relationships that flowered between them.

When Olmsted arrived in North Easton during the late summer of 1881 to design the grounds for the Ames Memorial Hall, he found the building nearing completion on its granite ledge, high above the street. No effort had been made to groom this restless site to accommodate the building. On the contrary, it was the building that yielded to the ledge; its rugged granite walls seemed to be an organic extension of the living rock. Granite outcroppings were a pervasive feature of the New England landscape, symbolic in their outbursts of the underlying strengths of the region, yet this was the first time in Richardson's developing career that he had the opportunity to work with a site in which the dynamics of nature were so aggressively present. The sheer energy of his response reveals more than his profound sensitivity to granite: in the depth to which it probes the nature of materials, it is not without its transcendental overtones. Ralph Waldo Emerson reminds us that in late-nineteenth-century America, the elevated rocky ledge was seen as a natural platform for the transcendental experience. "The geologist lays bare the strata, and can tell them all on his fingers," he wrote, "but does he know what effect passes into the man who builds his house in them? what effect on the race that inhabits the granite shelf?" Then, reflecting on the "tranquil landscape" and the "distant line of the horizon," he added that "we are never tired, as long as we can see far enough."[1]

Neither Richardson nor Olmsted was a stranger to transcendental doctrine. Richardson could not have avoided it at Harvard, and as a Unitarian may even have embraced it, while Olmsted, in his search for truth in nature, was an avid reader of Emerson. Both men were also close friends of William Emerson, Ralph Waldo's passionately transcendental older brother, who had been their neighbor when they lived next to one another on Staten Island. Thus, when called on to design the stairs leading up the rocky outcropping to Richardson's building, Olmsted knew exactly what the architect had in mind: working closely with Richardson, he terraced the stairs in a series of flights that wound naturally through the undulating land and strengthened the organic connections between building and ledge; at the same time, he provided the horizontal base essential to the visual stability of the soaring arcaded façade. The rest of the area he left in its natural state, with only occasional new planting to fill the voids and quicken the qualities that gave it life.

To carry these natural qualities further into the heart of the town, Olmsted next turned his attention to the dangling triangle of land formed by the division of Main Street. Although the northern tip of this parcel was relatively flat, it rose sharply on its long southern side to form a lesser outcropping that was actually an upward thrust of the same bed of granite that held the Memorial Hall aloft and underlay the entire region. Olmsted transformed this awkward plot, which he referred to as the "Town Square," into a small public park with plantings, benches, and two levels of walk, the lower of which passed through the ridge beneath a rough stone arch. He softened its sharpness, asserting its contours. The steep side of the ridge, which faced the hall, he built up with unmortared fieldstones so that, in his words, "its general aspect may be consistent with the rock elevation of the Memorial Hall grounds."[2] By evoking the qualities and behavior of granite in its natural state, Olmsted joined building and park as the visual and material center of the town.

The remaining three buildings that Richardson designed for North Easton were commissioned by Frederick Lothrop Ames. The Old Colony Railroad Station came to the architect in November of 1881. Its primary function was, of course, practical: situated immediately adjacent to the shovel shops, yet readily accessible to the community at large (including the Ames estates), it provided a convenient gateway to the world beyond North Easton for both the company and the town. At the same time it brought the largeness and power of Richardson's architecture into a direct relationship with the working segment of the community. Its stone walls and horizontal profile bonded it with the shovel shops; its robust masonry and springing arches reached back to the library and Memorial Hall. By embracing both, it became a living symbol for the combined energies of the town; by opening North

Easton to the world beyond, it celebrated the contribution of the Ames family to the development of the railroad in the country as a whole.

The crowning moment in the saga of Richardson at North Easton is the gate lodge he designed for Langwater. The commission was received in his office in March of 1880, while Memorial Hall was still under construction. There can be no question that it was conceived by F. L. Ames and that his thinking and aspirations were constant factors in its development. It seems to have come under discussion as early as the winter of 1879, and because it was a project within a larger scheme to develop the northern part of the Langwater grounds, both Olmsted and Richardson were consulted. As the concept crystallized, however, two other artists were drawn in: the sculptor Augustus Saint-Gaudens and the decorator Louis Comfort Tiffany. The form that Ames's idea would ultimately take, therefore, was the work of four of the nation's most creative artists, and when it was finished all of those involved—including Ames himself—thought it of sufficient import to sign the building: a signature stone bearing the monogram of each was placed in the wall of the second-floor porch that occupied the northwest corner of the building.

The gate lodge was situated athwart the driveway, a short distance in from the street at the northern boundary of the estate. It was constructed of massive granite boulders with Longmeadow sandstone trim; its hipped and conical roofs were covered with red-orange tile. Although called the "gate lodge," it was planned to serve four functions, two in each of its two quite disparate parts. Crossing the driveway and extending to the east was an emphatically horizontal single-story unit. At its extreme western end were two gigantic stone arches, one in each wall, through which the driveway passed to form the gateway to the estate. Its second purpose was found behind its formidable walls, where a large, open space terminated on the eastern end in a voluminous circular alcove with a conical roof; the floor was dirt and the ceiling trussed, and it was illuminated by a continuous strip window that ran the entire length of the unit, just under the eaves. This remarkable space was used for the winter storage of plants and as a maintenance center for the gardens and grounds. In short, it was intended to serve F. L. Ames's interest in horticulture, an interest that took him into the planning and management of his own estate with the same specialist's concern that he gave to the Arnold Arboretum.

The other unit of the gate lodge abutted the great arches on the western side of the driveway. It was two stories high, and although it maintained a continuous wall facing the street, it penetrated the estate grounds more deeply and actively than did its easterly counterpart; it was also much more complicated in plan. The first floor provided living quarters for the gardener and housekeeper; the second contained four bedrooms and a "bachelor's hall," all clearly intended as a retreat for the sons of the family and their friends.

The term "bachelor's hall" might suggest that the space was seen as a whoopee room where the young men could let off steam without disturbing the decorum of the main house. F. L. Ames, however, was very much a man of his time and place, and this was the last thing he had in mind. His Unitarian commitment taught him that his beliefs were meaningless until they were brought to living reality in the everyday conduct of life, and he expected the same from his sons. The bachelor's hall was thus a fellowship hall where the

young men came to discuss, to argue, to question, to challenge, and in the end to strengthen personal bonds. But it also
had another and much more profound purpose. It was both a
crucible and a symbol of learning. Together with the two
spaces into which it flowed—a balustraded porch and beyond
that a fascinating round-ended well house—the hall formed a
special tripartite architectural entity that was programmed to
a common theme. The primary clue to that theme is found
where the well house joins the porch. Here, the support
between the top of the balustrade and the porch lintel is made
up of two short freestanding segments of a Greek Doric column, which together carry a flat, roughly cut stone slab.
Although seemingly incongruous amid the random energy of
the boulder walls, this highly rational element is the key to
the program: the two columns are the pillars of the earth, and
together with the slab they form an ancient symbol for the
earth itself. The building is, in fact, an ode to the earth and as
such addresses a major preoccupation of the late nineteenth
century. Under the scrutiny of the earth scientists, especially
the geologists, the earth was taking on a dramatic new identity that would change forever the way human beings thought
about the world in which they lived. It fired the American
curiosity just as space has captured the imagination in the late
twentieth century, and F. L. Ames was one of those deeply
involved. His gift to his sons, to encourage their curiosity, was
the gate lodge, and in view of his ardent interest in horticulture it must have been a great source of satisfaction for him
that his youngest son, John, received a master's degree in den-
drology from Harvard.

The thematic development generates around the pillars of
the earth. Immediately across from that motif, and also fram-

ing the entrance to the well house, is another post, this time square and rising from floor to lintel. On this post are reliefs by Saint-Gaudens; there are also reliefs in the bachelor's hall on the mantel over the fireplace in the inglenook; on the chimney breast are decorative tiles by Tiffany. Together, these various displays evoke the four ancient elements—earth, air, fire, and water. In the well house, water and air combine to produce life-giving moisture; in the inglenook, fire and air combine to give life-sustaining warmth. On the floor of the porch and at the foot of the post with the Saint-Gaudens carvings is an ancient symbol of procreation, a large stone frog with a small frog on its back, also by Saint-Gaudens. In other words, the bachelor's hall combines with its two appendages to create a reflective space that ponders ancient theories of the earth and of the origins of life itself. The ideas of the Pythagoreans and Aristotle seem to dominate the thinking, which is precisely what one would expect from a man educated at Exeter and Harvard.

In contrast to the contemplative quiet of the bachelor's hall, the main thrust of the building is dynamic, even aggressive. Conceived in the same direct physical terms as those that marked the thinking of the leading earth scientists and philosophers of the day, Richardson's brilliant statement was at the cutting edge of his time and had several commanding voices in its support—Asa Gray, Louis Agassiz, Charles Darwin, Ralph Waldo Emerson—all well-known to him and to Ames and Olmsted. The most directly formative voice, however, was that of the English critic and writer John Ruskin. An amateur geologist of considerable distinction, as well as a devout evangelical Christian, Ruskin's critical judgment was formed by his scientific discoveries as well as by his legendary biblical knowledge. At the very heart of his criticism is the notion that all art must be based on truth in nature, whether it is revealed by science or the Bible. The strong Unitarian overtones of this concept are obvious, but it was also his broad appeal to nature that made his writings widely attractive in the United States. To relate those truths to architecture, Ruskin (in *Stones of Venice*) uses one of the most famous mountains in the world, the Matterhorn, as a metaphor for a building, analyzing its walls, buttresses, peaks, and ridge lines all as natural forms that lie at the root of architecture. Later (in *Modern Painters*, vol. 4), in an effort to reconcile geological truth with the biblical account of creation, he goes further and seeks to define the role of the mountain in the grand cycle of life on earth. He recognizes that the mountain was elevated by mighty forces "we know not of," and then argues that this was done to make water flow, to make air move, and to generate storms that form the glaciers. These, in turn, grind the fragments of stone that fall from the mountain to form the silt that is then carried by the streams and rivers to the valley below, where it mixes with vegetable matter to create life-giving soil.

It is this organic vision that lies behind the gate lodge. Both Richardson and Olmsted had read Ruskin carefully, the latter ardently, and there can be no question of the Englishman's influence on Richardson's design. Although it was the architect's fertile imagination, responding in total sympathy, that gave the building its shape and character, the imprint of Ruskin's account is simply too evident at too many points to be denied. But Richardson turned the tables on Ruskin, making the building the metaphor for the mountain. The gate lodge is a mountain in miniature, in effect a living organism with its internal energies contained and directed by its walls and buttresses, peaks and slopes, cornices and caves, each pressing to shape its ever-changing profile. The gigantic arches that spring from the ground to span the driveway symbolize those mighty forces that have lifted the mountain to its destiny in the clouds; the massive glacial boulders that form the walls stand for the life-giving cycle of events that were put in motion by the mountain. Together they are the energy that animates the building, giving it a vitality beyond its physical presence and meaning beyond its function.

The Ames Gate Lodge is a ringing affirmation of the earth as a living organism and of the countless forms of life that are its glory. As a proclamation of belief on the part of F. L. Ames, its liberal vision is Unitarian to the core. But Ames's faith also taught him that the physical world he could see, and of which he was a living part, was created and empowered by a God he could not see. To contemplate nature was thus one way to experience God. Acutely sensitive to the inwardness of this most private of acts, Richardson created a serene and isolated space where it could take place. Corbeled out from the side of the well house is a heavy slab of granite that forms a tiny balcony, given access through the narrow passage between the pillars of the earth and the pier with the Saint-Gaudens reliefs. Rich with symbolism and hovering above the splendor of the Olmsted grounds, this elevated point is surely Emerson's "granite shelf" from which the Ames sons could look out over "the tranquil landscape" to "the distant line of the horizon" and be one with their God.

The fifth building in North Easton designed by Richardson was a small shingle-style gardener's cottage. It was commissioned by F. L. Ames in March of 1884, four years after the gate lodge, and was located a short distance to the east, near the southeast corner of the Langwater estate. It was obviously an adjunct to the gate lodge, made necessary by the continuing development and management of the Olmsted grounds. Although much less aggressive than the gate lodge and more gentle in texture, it has the same contained energy and largeness that emanate from every building Richardson ever designed. Even though it is small, to see it is not a pianissimo experience. Rather, viewing it is like listening to a great operatic baritone singing full voice, but offstage. Although diminished in volume, the timbre and vitality are still there. This little wooden gem closed the chapter on Richardson's work at North Easton: the architect died two years later, in 1886, just eighty-three years after Old Oliver established his first shovel shop.

Shortly after Richardson's death, American architecture began its turbulent transition toward the Modern Movement: the steel frame took over from stone masonry in construction, and the machine replaced the human hand in refining the building. Architects such as Richardson, whose work was born of the earth and rich in its material offerings, went out of favor and were even held in disdain. With Richardson thus silenced, life in North Easton continued in a form and at a pace uniquely its own, and his work settled quietly but proudly into the rhythms of the town. In the world outside North Easton, however, the Richardson buildings were largely forgotten, and they remained so for half a century until the Museum of Modern Art in New York mounted an exhibition of the architect's work to celebrate the fiftieth anniversary of his death. The show was motivated in part by the writings of the social historian Lewis Mumford, whose book *The Brown*

Decades (1931) was the first twentieth-century study of American culture to pay serious attention to Richardson as a major architect of his time. The exhibition was accompanied in 1936 by Henry-Russell Hitchcock's now-seminal work, *The Architecture of H. H. Richardson and His Times.* Hitchcock played an active role in the preparation of the exhibition, and his book was conceived as part of its offering. Together, they presented Richardson as the precursor of the Modern Movement. This not only provoked a lively interest in his work, particularly among the professional architects and critics, but in the end it also brought North Easton back into critical regard. Hitchcock paid careful attention to Richardson's work there, especially the gate lodge, and his insights opened the way for the second chapter of the North Easton story.

Shortly after the publication of Hitchcock's book, World War II intervened to upset the lives of most Americans, and those in North Easton were no exception. In the decades following the war, however, interest in Richardson was renewed, especially among a group of young postwar scholars, and North Easton began to feel the impact of that interest. The gate lodge in particular attracted enthusiastic attention. Indeed, according to Mrs. John S. Ames, Jr., whose husband was a grandson of Frederick Lothrop Ames, the family was increasingly "besieged with requests to see the Gate Lodge by people from Holland, Norway, France, Germany, California, Harvard, Yale, etc., etc.—the Ames Family [has] been doing their best to perpetuate their heritage and [to meet] their responsibilities. However, having lived always with these various structures, it is bewildering to find they are of some sort of importance to others. Perhaps we need a better understanding more than the public, and certainly an exposure to knowledgeable, respected authorities on the subject."[3] The response of the family was intelligent and friendly, but over time the continuing requests to visit, study, and photograph the Richardson buildings became more and more of a burden. This was compounded in the 1960s by another event that finally prompted the Ameses to take concrete action: the Richardson railroad station, which was owned by the Old Colony Railroad, was put up for sale. The family entered a bid and ultimately bought and gave it to the Easton Historical Society, which now runs it as a museum. At the time, however, the matter was still up in the air, and to help the family better to understand and cope with their growing problems, a daylong tour of all the Richardson buildings was organized that opened them to visitors. Planned and led by Mrs. John S. Ames, Jr., and sponsored by the Oakes Ames Memorial Hall Association, of which Mrs. Ames was president, this "First H. H. Richardson Tour" was held on 12 October 1968. To give substance to the day, five of the current leading Richardson scholars were invited to lecture on various aspects of the master's work. Heading the list was Henry-Russell Hitchcock himself, who was then at the height of his career. He was followed by four younger men: Vincent Scully from Yale; William Jordy from Brown; Lawrence Homolka, a former graduate student of Hitchcock's then teaching at Emory University; and myself from Williams College. Four of the lectures were held in the Oakes Ames Memorial Hall: Homolka's and Hitchcock's were in the morning, those of Jordy and Scully in the afternoon; I talked throughout the day to periodic groups at the gate lodge.

Altogether, this first public effort was a memorable occasion—rich in ideas, brightened by the grace of the Ames family, and blessed with the sunshine of a brilliant autumn day. But it also provided the Ameses with an incentive for a more efficient and professional management of the Richardson buildings. During the decades that followed, significant restoration and maintenance work was carried out, not only on those buildings but also on the original shops to freshen their appearance and reaffirm the bonds between the shops, Richardson's work, and Olmsted's landscaping.

To celebrate these accomplishments and to gather ideas and support for the future, the Oakes Ames Memorial Hall Association sponsored a second public event, but this time at a more ambitious and professional level. It was a three-day program with wide cultural reach, supported as it was by the Ames Free Library, the Children's Museum of Easton, the Easton Cultural Council, the Easton Historical Society, and Unity Church. It opened on Friday evening, 27 September 1996, with a gala reception at Langwater. Saturday was devoted to learning and the exchange of ideas: a colloquium in the morning; walking tours and lectures in the afternoon, followed by tea at the Ames Free Library; and in the evening a birthday party for H. H. Richardson. On Sunday there was a bus tour of selected Richardson works in the Boston area.

The colloquium was the heart of the festival. In contrast to the informal nature of the earlier meeting, this one was highly structured, with papers all addressing the common theme, "The Legacy of H. H. Richardson, 1996." The panelists were from the younger generation of Richardson scholars, and the papers that were delivered on that morning form the content of this book. It is the first effort on the part of the Ames family to contribute to the scholarship on Richardson and as such is a living tribute to their intelligent and steadfast commitment to their precious heritage. But it also adds fresh meaning to the searching declaration of belief that Frederick Lothrop Ames and H. H. Richardson were able to weave into the fabric of the gate lodge. It is singularly appropriate that the member of the Ames family who organized the 1996 festival and managed this publication is a great-grandson of his revered ancestor and bears the same name. The current Frederick Lothrop Ames combines the curiosity of a first-class historian with a devotion to family and to their Unitarian commitment to truth. He has an unbiased but sympathetic understanding of their role in the shaping and opening of the American land; and he is particularly sensitive to their efforts to enhance a special portion of that land through the expressive power of architecture and landscape design. By his dedication to and support of both the 1996 festival and this publication, he has helped to bring fresh energy to the inexhaustible life of North Easton and to ensure its preservation for generations to come.

Notes

1. Ralph Waldo Emerson, "Beauty," in *The Conduct of Life* (Boston: Ticknor and Fields, 1860); and "Nature" (1836), in *The Portable Emerson*, ed. Carl Bode and Malcolm Cowley (New York: Penguin, 1981), 11, 14.

2. "DFT, April 10, 1882, Brookline," container 17, folder 4, FLO Papers; cited by Robert F. Brown, "The Aesthetic Transformation of an Industrial Community," *Winterthur Portfolio* 12 (1977): 47.

3. Mrs. John S. Ames, Jr., letter to Vincent Scully, 18 July 1968. Copy in author's files.

·

WILLIAM H.
PIERSON, JR.

H. H. Richardson

THE PICTURESQUE IN
the DESIGN METHOD OF
H. H. RICHARDSON:
Memorial Hall,
North Easton

1

Thomas C. Hubka

For over one hundred years, H. H. Richardson's buildings have been described as Romanesque by historians who have emphasized the architect's powerful medieval forms.[1] For modernist historians such as Henry-Russell Hitchcock, who attempted to look beyond the Romanesque label, certain Richardson buildings were singled out as precursors of the Modern Movement. But while a number of these designs were praised, others represented a romantic eclecticism and a lingering stylistic historicism. Especially troubling were Richardson's many asymmetrical, nonformal compositions. These picturesque buildings, such as the Oakes Ames Memorial Hall (1879–1881; fig. 1.1) in North Easton,

·

Thomas C.

Hubka

1.1.

H. H. Richardson, Oakes Ames
Memorial Hall, North Easton,
Mass., 1879–1881. Photo from
Mariana Griswold Van Rensselaer,
Henry Hobson Richardson and His Works
(Boston: Houghton Mifflin, 1888).

Massachusetts, were particularly distasteful to modernists, who lamented their immense popularity during the nineteenth century and the subsequent spread of what they considered to be the worst characteristics of the Richardsonian Romanesque throughout the United States.[2]

Recently scholars have emphasized a more complex underlying significance to Richardson's works, including his picturesque compositions, but there has been little agreement about the merits of these picturesque solutions. Most observers would agree, however, that even at its most picturesque, Richardson's architecture rarely suffered from an undisciplined Victorian eclecticism. As James F. O'Gorman has forcefully argued, Richardson's ability "to discipline the picturesque" and to provide an underlying order to his vigorous compositions contributed significantly to his greatness.[3] That ability distinguished him from even his best Victorian contemporaries. When his buildings are analyzed as solutions that evolved from a sequence of steps in design development, they consistently reveal Richardson's attempt to use the logic and order of the plan to tame and discipline his muscular massing and picturesque compositions.[4] Most historians have identified his academic training at the Ecole des Beaux-Arts as the source for his understanding of the importance and rationality of the plan to control decision making about design. Yet this standard interpretation of Richardson's strategy can adequately explain the three-dimensional massing only of those projects—like the Allegheny County Courthouse, Pittsburgh (1883–1888)—that are dominated by the expression of the plan. If we were to analyze many more of Richardson's designs solely through the perspective of his Ecole des Beaux-Arts training and the rational expression of the plan, we would have no way of understanding the development of their massing and elevations. In particular, we would have little way of accounting for projects such as his North Easton commissions, which abound in irregular, nonformalistic solutions that are not predicted by their plan development.

This paper examines the meaning of those Richardson buildings exhibiting what I describe as "picturesque" characteristics, including structures with asymmetrical, romantic, Gothic, or nonformal features. Such a classification of Richardson's works poses considerable difficulties, both because the definition of the picturesque in Richardson's work is complex and because picturesque and formal characteristics coexist in much of his work. Nevertheless, we must recognize the recurrence of these picturesque characteristics in many of Richardson's works, such as his North Easton buildings and particularly the Memorial Hall, which have not been seen as reflecting a unified design strategy. Far from being aberrations or temporary lapses among his works, these buildings and their vigorous picturesque massing were the product of one of Richardson's principal design strategies. Frequently, they have not been ranked among Richardson's finest work because, when compared to formal, rationalistic, Ecole des Beaux-Arts-influenced solutions, they appear to be loosely organized and to lack a formal design strategy. Yet they are not the product of an undisciplined picturesqueness: these picturesque solutions result from a highly developed, coherent strategy.

We could maintain that these "irregular" or picturesque projects, so detested by influential critics such as Hitchcock, either revealed the picturesque infatuation of a maturing architect soon to be cured of the excesses of youth or displayed the inconsistencies of a master too busy with other projects late in his career.[5] Although neither of these once widely accepted hypotheses is now convincing, current studies still provide only vague, usually negative, summaries of the picturesque buildings, and certainly nothing approaching an articulated design philosophy has been proposed to explain their development and to evaluate their merits. They include some of Richardson's finest nonformalist works, such as the Sherman, Stoughton, and Glessner houses (1874, 1882, and 1885); the Ames and Crane libraries (1877 and 1880); Brattle Square Church (1881); and the Ames Gate Lodge (1880); as well as many nonsymmetrical, nonformalistic portions of his other major designs, such Austin Hall (1881), the Rectory for Trinity Church (1879), and the Paine house (1883). When we carefully examine the design development of these solutions, we will see that Richardson employed standard patterns of nonformal or "picturesque" design that constituted a type of personal design strategy. These underlying principles of picturesque design, or principles of the sublime (as John Ruskin might have labeled them), can be recognized in approximately half of his total buildings—those buildings most fully characterized by functional expression and asymmetrical organization and massing. Such methods were not unique to Richardson and were employed by other architects of his era, who produced nonformal, picturesque designs. Richardson's distinct genius was to integrate these tendencies with his formal methods.

CONTEXT

Before we analyze Richardson's picturesque design strategy, we need to consider three issues related to this topic: the term *picturesque,* the historical view of Richardson's work, and the rational foundation of Richardson's approach to design. First, the word itself is both awkward and controversial. Despite a quarter century of postmodern reevaluation, the modernist disdain for the idea of the picturesque (associated with narrative in literature) still clouds the term and renders it highly suspect in any artistic context.[6] In a neutral climate, *picturesque* might communicate an artistic work's rich variety of forms or symbolism, frequently associated with the varieties of nature as so often demonstrated in genre and landscape paintings from the nineteenth century. Although today the term may be used positively, it most often conveys an insubstantiality and lack of artistic depth. For example, within the architectural profession, a design called picturesque is often viewed with disfavor as a sign of undisciplined excess.[7] But despite these limitations, the word is uniquely appropriate for conveying a nineteenth-century positivism and optimism about the possibilities of a nature-inspired architecture full of rich variety and even evocative of myth and legend. From this more optimistic perspective, I wish to demonstrate that the concept of the picturesque and its related design methods were fundamental to many of Richardson's greatest works.

Second, Henry-Russell Hitchcock's groundbreaking scholarship continues to influence Richardsonian studies more than sixty years after its publication. In most respects, Hitchcock's studies have stood the test of time; but certain areas, such as his consistent championship of Richardson as a precursor of the Modern Movement and his dismissal of nineteenth-century English influences in Richardson's work, have required considerable reevaluation. For our purposes here, Hitchcock's refusal to consider a Ruskinian/High Victorian/English medieval revival influence on Richardson is most troubling.[8] (Although Hitchcock attempted to revise his original

assessment of Ruskin's influence in later publications, these efforts should be seen as highly inadequate and self-serving.[9])
Hitchcock's intense dislike of Richardson's most picturesque, "Ruskinian" buildings, such as Memorial Hall, has had, and continues to have, an immense influence that has only recently begun to be reassessed. For example, Hitchcock briefly dismissed Memorial Hall as "an awkward and aggressive pile," describing it as "unsuccessful as architecture," "a lapse and almost an anachronism," and "unworthy of Richardson's genius."[10] Within this climate of hostility, dictated by one of America's greatest architectural historians, it is not surprising that little attention has been paid to Memorial Hall and related works that share picturesque characteristics.

Third, although I will present the picturesque conceptions underlying Richardson's designs, I by no means understate the fundamental importance of both his Ecole des Beaux-Arts training and the underlying rationalism of his plan development. As every major Richardsonian scholar has observed, these characteristics are the starting point for any discussion of his design strategy.[11] This analysis is valid even for those solutions with picturesque massing. Nevertheless, I am simultaneously emphasizing that in many of his "picturesque" designs, his training is insufficient to account for the underlying principles or beliefs that sustained and motivated Richardson in their development. Or to state it more succinctly, you cannot get from the Ecole des Beaux-Arts to Memorial Hall, and you cannot get from the plan of Memorial Hall to its massing and elevations. Other design ideas besides those derived from his French architectural education, with its emphasis on the formal plan and the symmetrical elevation, must have been employed by Richardson.

Memorial Hall warrants close analysis both because it is a significant example of Richardson's picturesque work and because, in the wake of Hitchcock's negative assessment, it deserves a fairer review. To his credit, Hitchcock identified genuine weaknesses in its design.[12] But whatever else we may say about Memorial Hall, it is not, as Hitchcock either stated or implied, the product of a distracted, overworked, poorly staffed, or dying architect—assessments that were also applied to Richardson's later picturesque works. It is rather the disciplined product of one of America's finest architects approaching the height of his short but amazingly fruitful career. Furthermore, the project was aided by an amiable client, a loose program (which allowed the architect considerable freedom), a skillful builder, and more than adequate assistants, including Frederick Law Olmsted. We therefore must conclude that Richardson produced the building he fully desired. In other words, Memorial Hall was not a picturesque mistake but the fully considered work of an acknowledged master at the peak of creative powers. For these reasons, Memorial Hall is worthy of careful examination to reveal insights into the design method of its architect.

MEMORIAL HALL, NORTH EASTON, MASSACHUSETTS

One way to analyze Memorial Hall is to place the building within a typological grouping of Richardson's works. This approach has been pioneered by James O'Gorman, who has significantly deepened our understanding of how to classify the buildings. O'Gorman's insistence on functional grouping has encouraged a multilevel analysis of Richardson's works by recognizing that a large part of the architect's genius was his ability to bring fundamentally different types of solutions and styles to different types of architectural problems.[13] Previous critics had usually classified the works either by their Romanesque stylistic characteristics or, following Hitchcock's lead, by the degree to which they predicted modernist tendencies.

Within the complete record of architectural history, Richardson is probably unparalleled in the creation of brilliant, prototype designs to address different architectural problems. These include new types of solutions for urban housing (the Glessner house), the commuter rail station (North Easton and others), the modern commercial building (Marshall Field Wholesale Store), the suburban library (Crane Library and others), the vacation house (the Sherman house), and the urban government center (Allegheny County Courthouse). Such multifunctional design creativity, with different typological solutions (and occasionally different styles) offered for different types of functional problems, is paradoxically unlike the results of modern functionalism, which proposed similar types and styles of solutions for different kinds of problems.

By employing this type of premodern, functional evaluation, we can see Memorial Hall not just as a picturesque Romanesque building but as an experiment in the creation of a new type of building solution (fig. 1.2). Memorial Hall was Richardson's well-considered approach to the problem of creating a new type of small-town government building for the American suburban community. To his American audience it seemed radical, for it was not like typical American civic buildings of the period; instead, it drew on European romantic medieval-vernacular imagery, and in particular the European raised town hall. Once before, in a captivating sketch for the Brookline, Massachusetts, Town Hall project (1870; fig. 1.3),

I.2.

H. H. RICHARDSON, Memorial Hall.
Photo from *The Architecture of Henry
Hobson Richardson in North Easton,
Massachusetts* ([North Easton,
Mass.]: Oakes Ames Memorial Hall
Association and Easton Historical
Society, 1969).

———————

Richardson had proposed a raised-hall municipal building, based on European medieval models, but Memorial Hall was his first realization of this design.

Civic buildings with major second-floor meeting rooms were not unknown in New England, where citizens were constructing halls for town meetings during the years before the Civil War. For example, Lyceum Hall in Winchester,

1.3.

H. H. RICHARDSON, Brookline Town
Hall project, Brookline, Mass., 1870.
From Van Rensselaer, *Henry Hobson
Richardson.*

Massachusetts (1851), was designed with a major second-floor
meeting room with commercial space below (fig. 1.4).[14] In
developing this building type, however, Richardson more
closely followed the model of the medieval raised hall, which
had a crofted or vaulted understory expressed on the exterior in
the form of an arcade. This vaulted form of European town hall
was one of the most common types of medieval civic buildings
(fig 1.5).[15] The powerful arcades of the ground floors at
Memorial Hall and the Brookline Town Hall project, support-

1.4.

THEODORE VOELCKERS, Lyceum
Hall, Winchester, Mass., 1851. Photo
courtesy of the Winchester, Mass.,
Archival Center.

ing large second-floor rooms, closely follow these European precedents. Richardson's selection of a European vernacular source, which probably represented a historical pattern well known to him from both his European study and medieval revival literature, was typical of his eclectic borrowing from various European medieval precedents. The roots of Richardson's preference for such European solutions are not well known, but they are slowly being acknowledged by scholars including the late Margaret Henderson Floyd and William H. Pierson, Jr.[16] For example, Floyd has demonstrated that the same type of medieval vernacular precedent used at Memorial Hall occurred at the Glessner house, which incorporated into its design the forms present in a French vernacular manor house, Manoir d'Ango.[17]

1.5.

Kaufthaus, Freiburg, Germany, fifteenth century. Photo from *European
Architecture* 5 (October 1896–October
1897).

One of the characteristics of medieval vernacular architecture that attracted architects of Richardson's generation was
the juxtaposition of various styles and periods in an eclectic
manner. This approach contrasts with an earlier, pre–Civil War
Gothic revival, as seen in the works of Richard Upjohn, who
copied medieval forms more faithfully and less creatively.[18] At
Memorial Hall, one example of this vernacular eclecticism may
be found on the north side in the surprising juxtaposition of
the wooden vernacular dormer and its wooden gallery above
rugged Richardsonian masonry (see fig. 1.1). On the front
façade, one finds another example in the common brick set
above the monumental rusticated stone arcade, a contrast that
is reinforced by the purposeful asymmetry of the major façade.

These elements of romantic, vernacular eclecticism were what Hitchcock, the unrelenting modernist, singled out for scathing criticism. While this robust visual eclecticism of the Memorial Hall solution was widely copied in town halls throughout America, the typological model of the two-story European town hall was not. Therefore, unlike his successful new prototypes for the commuter railroad station and the small-town library, it was a solution that was not followed, although, as Hitchcock lamented, its architectural style was widely copied.

PICTURESQUE CHARACTERISTICS IN RICHARDSON'S WORK

In adopting the design concept of a medieval European town hall, Richardson produced a unique building; however, it followed a pattern of design development that he had employed in many of his more picturesque projects. Elsewhere I have described the design strategies Richardson employed for two of his finest nonformal buildings, the Glessner and Sherman houses, and these buildings will provide a framework for interpreting the design decisions about Memorial Hall, of which little is known.

I have argued in previous analyses that many of the underlying ideas behind Richardson's projects exhibiting "picturesque" characteristics may be more accurately understood by reference to John Ruskin's ideas and influences.[19] Without addressing the tantalizing issue of Richardson's direct knowledge of, or direct influence by, Ruskinian ideas, I consider Ruskinian ideas a valuable interpretive framework in assessing Richardson's design decisions for those projects, like Memorial Hall, exhibiting nonformalistic, asymmetrical, or picturesque characteristics. Although I will focus on Memorial Hall, I believe that various picturesque works by Richardson share a common attitude or set of design principles that suggest a personal design strategy. Guiding his overall design development was an orientation to nineteenth-century picturesque or romantic design that implicitly constitutes a body of design principles, strategies, or rules of thumb that continually recur in most of his "picturesque" works. Because Richardson did not write or otherwise communicate with others about his design method, these principles cannot definitively be attributed to the writings of Ruskin, although they are closely aligned with Ruskinian philosophy and sources.[20] Together, these Ruskinian principles, or "principles of the picturesque," either in part or whole underlie Richardson's design method for picturesque structures such as Memorial Hall, whether or not they were derived directly from Ruskinian sources. I will confine my analysis mainly to Memorial Hall, although I believe that many of Richardson's projects were guided by the same design principles.

FUNCTIONALISM

The clarity and simplicity of the typical Richardsonian plan are apparent from the published plans for Memorial Hall (fig. 1.6.) Yet they provide little hint of the eclectic massing and visual excitement of the exterior, a dynamic contrast typical of most of Richardson's picturesque solutions. Those two fundamental forms of architectural thinking, the plan and the elevation, were in essence kept separate. In this respect, Richardson was no different from most of his leading Victorian contemporaries, as may be seen in a comparison of equivalently scaled plans and elevations by Frank Furness, Richard Morris Hunt, George Edmund Street, and William Burges.[21]

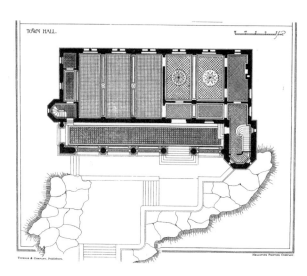

1.6.

H. H. RICHARDSON, Memorial Hall.
First-floor plan. From *The Architecture
of Richardson in North Easton.*

The critical question concerning the relationship between
the plan and massing employed by Richardson and architects
who similarly produced picturesque compositions is not easily
summarized because they did not follow clearly specified geo-
metrical patterns or "correct" systems of classical proportion.
Like Richardson, who never articulated his design methods,
these Victorian architects did not explicitly set out for later
generations the rules, principles, or ideology of their design
method. But this silence does not mean that such principles
and method were absent.[22]

Through their many works, A. W. N. Pugin and, to a
much greater degree, Ruskin can be credited with articulating

a philosophy of architecture that obviously nourished the architects of Richardson's generation. These architectural theories were often based on first-hand interpretations of specific medieval buildings (for Pugin, English examples, and for Ruskin, Italian examples), and both reacted against the composed regularities of rational, classical, or post-Raphaelite designs and the overall effects of the industrial revolution. Both championed an idealized view of medieval civilization and the healing effects of nature and naturalistic imagery.[23]

Ruskin's analysis of the "noble irregularities" of the Gothic church plan best encapsulates his and Pugin's complex approach to the ideal concept of the plan and its massing. They both understood that the underlying regularity of the plan in medieval churches was adjusted and expanded over time to produce an organized but frequently asymmetrical, picturesque beauty. Such an orientation was vividly expressed, for example, in Pugin's churches, such as St. Giles's, Cheadle (1840–1846), where the vigorous internal symmetry of the nave gives way to a spirited exterior complexity created by the juxtaposition of various functional elements such as the chancel, aisles, porches, and tower. Through their detailed studies of medieval precedents, Pugin and Ruskin reinforced a medievalist conception of functional expression in which the irregularities of plan were "honestly expressed" in the massing and elevation of the buildings.[24]

Many of Richardson's picturesque works clearly took inspiration from this Gothic-functionalist type of interior-exterior interpretation, as he expressed the difference in room organization and usage in the exterior massing and detailing of his buildings. Richardson follows this strategy on the front façade of Memorial Hall, where he articulates the various components of the plan: the isolated stair tower, the separate articulation of the minor stage area (second floor, left side), and the larger meeting hall underneath the larger hipped roof (see fig. 1.2).

Such an approach differs significantly from interpretations of functionalism today. Unlike modernists after 1920, who relied on a unified style to minimize the differences in functional expression of the program, the medieval revival functionalists (guided by the theories of Pugin and Ruskin) attempted to exaggerate the contrast in functional expression and to juxtapose separately articulated masses on the façade. This exaggeration is precisely Richardson's aim in the major façade at North Easton and his many other picturesque projects. Needless to say, Hitchcock, the consummate modernist, had little sympathy for this type of Gothic-functionalist expression and found the various subsidiary forms and asymmetrical expression at Memorial Hall confusing and lacking in aesthetic discipline. Whatever our opinion of the success of the façade, I believe it accurately reflected Richardson's "Gothic" functional expression of the irregularities of the plan, "honestly" expressed, as articulated by Pugin and Ruskin and as interpreted by most of his Victorian contemporaries. To the modernist, that approach is a prescription for visual chaos, but to the Ruskinian, deploying picturesque principles, the exterior of Memorial Hall is a logical, Gothically balanced expression of internal function.

HIERARCHY

In one of his most influential design directives, Ruskin states: "To compose is to arrange unequal things, and the first thing is to determine the principal thing. . . . Have one large thing and several smaller things, and bind them well together."[25]

Richardson's design for Memorial Hall is a textbook example of Ruskin's directive to bind a hierarchy of diverse parts into a unified whole. In the main elevation, the second-floor meeting room is clearly expressed as the building's dominant room by the towering roof and the major windows. The arcade, the stage area, and the stair tower are bound together as secondary, supportive elements. A similar strategy of unified compositional hierarchy was employed in Richardson's greatest asymmetrical designs, such as Crane Library, the Sherman house, and the Ames Gate Lodge. Richardson's overall intent for these picturesque designs reflects Ruskin's definition of the principles of Gothic proportion and composition: "One member of the composition must be either larger than, or in some way supreme, over the rest. There is no proportion between equal things. . . . [To] compose is to arrange unequal things."[26]

In Crane Library, in Quincy, Massachusetts, Richardson perhaps most successfully bound these separate, diverse elements together into a unified picturesque whole (fig. 1.7). While the Crane Library façade is almost universally recognized as one of Richardson's greatest works, the building is not often analyzed, as it should be, as a juxtaposition of unequal parts that creates a masterpiece of the picturesque composition. Hitchcock's strained efforts to find proto-modern tendencies in elements of the façade is an embarrassing attempt to avoid discussing its powerful asymmetrical composition. At Memorial Hall, which was designed one year earlier than Crane Library, Richardson was developing this same strategy of juxtaposition. And although the result at North Easton was less satisfying, the two buildings followed the same composition method.

1.7.

H. H. RICHARDSON, Thomas Crane
Library, Quincy, Mass., 1880. Photo
from Van Rensselaer, *Henry Hobson
Richardson.*

BALANCE

While the idea of hierarchy explains the variety of forms in a Richardsonian picturesque design, the idea of picturesque balance explains its unity and order. Ruskinian balance is central to his complex architectural aesthetic and perhaps the most important principle of the picturesque. This characteristic was derived by Ruskin from medieval precedents and especially from his observations of nature; he observed, for example, that no two sides of a leaf or a tree are identical, yet they are always harmoniously balanced. The principle of balance was reinforced by its frequent occurrence in medieval buildings; in such structures as the Doge's Palace, Venice, and Amiens Cathedral, cited by Ruskin, the subtle, unequal sides of a façade produce balanced compositions.[27] This strategy became an absolute mainstay of nineteenth-century medieval revival designers seeking the type of balance inspired by nature and confirmed in the asymmetrical façades of Gothic buildings, particularly churches with different towers. To a Ruskinian "Goth," the asymmetrical façade of a medieval cathedral such as Chartres is perfectly balanced. Asymmetrical balance can similarly be observed in most of Richardson's picturesque designs, including Memorial Hall, where the vertical stair tower on the north is "balanced" by the short gable extension and extended arcade on the south.

By examining the drawings for Austin Hall (1881), Billings Library (1883), and portions of the Glessner house (1885), for which—unlike Memorial Hall and Crane Library—extensive design development drawings exist, we can observe Richardson's quest for this Gothic balance.[28] Substituting the idea of balance for the classical beaux-arts goal of symmetry, Richardson carefully seeks the balance of unequal parts. This mature strategy of design was not part of Richardson's Ecole des Beaux-Arts training. It was, however, a distinct characteristic of those designers, like his English contemporaries pursuing the medieval revival, who attempted to achieve a "Gothic," creative balance in their building façades.

NATURE AS SOURCE

Of all Ruskin's teachings that were to affect the course of architectural development during the second half of the nineteenth century, none was so broadly influential as his insistence that nature be the fundamental source for art and architectural design. Although practically all architectural theory up to Ruskin's era acknowledged nature as a significant reference point for design, Ruskin vitalized this belief with a medievalist bias. As a result of his writings, generations of nineteenth- and early twentieth-century architects believed that truth in architecture was both inspired by nature and confirmed in Gothic buildings, which they interpreted as embodying such inspiration.

Victorian architects were particularly responsive to Ruskin's emphasis on nature's multiplicities and its "subtle varieties." Ruskin had observed subtle visual irregularities and asymmetries in nature, including geological formations, which he saw reproduced in his favorite medieval buildings, such as St. Mark's and the Doge's Palace. He chastised those architects (including Pugin) who mechanically developed buildings without obeying principles present in nature's own forms: "You know how fond modern architects are of their equalities, and similarities; how necessary they think it that every part of a building should be like every other part. Nature abhors equality and similitude just as foolish men love them."[29] These naturalistic themes become central components of

Richardson's picturesque design philosophy. At Memorial Hall, as in most of his buildings, each capital of the major arcade columns is treated differently. Overall, Ruskin's directive to study nature defines an important aesthetic ideology in which the designer develops a solution incorporating subtle balancing and nonsymmetrical, nonmechanical, nonrepetitive organization.

THE SUBLIME

Although not the first to champion the sublime in architecture, Ruskin provided a forceful, definitive articulation of one of the most powerful design directives of the nineteenth century. Through many reworkings of his theories, he continued to stress that one strain of architectural beauty could be found in the power, strength, and ruggedness observed in nature. Even a casual observer of Richardson's work is repeatedly struck by the force of his rugged, naturalistic expression, which most commentators have assumed was Richardson's attempt to distill nature's powerful forces into his trademark expression of a bold, lithic monumentality. This expression of the sublime is evident in his North Easton projects, especially the Ames Gate Lodge (fig. 1.8), which is one of the most powerful expressions of American sublime naturalism ever produced. Richardson was, however, only one of many American practitioners of this sublime naturalism. Others included Andrew Jackson Downing, A. J. Davis, Calvert Vaux, and Olmsted, who all acknowledged that Ruskin's writings on nature profoundly influenced their work.[30]

A specific design strategy inspired by Ruskinian ideas about nature that influenced picturesque designs such as Memorial Hall is the concept of "natural growth." That a

1.8.

H. H. Richardson, Ames Gate
Lodge, North Easton, Mass., 1880.
Photo from *The Architecture of*
Richardson in North Easton.

building should reflect and reveal how it physically grows and
ages is a central Gothic-romantic ideal. Ruskin gave powerful
support to this idea by emphasizing the relationship of rugged
mountain imagery and medieval buildings such as St. Mark's,
which was added to over time and which conveyed the qualities of age, textural variety, and rugged strength.[31] At
Memorial Hall, the building grows outward and upward like a
romantic castle on a granite mountain (see fig. 1.1). The entry
sequence is a tour de force of naturalistic ascent: a dramatically
staged progression from a rocky, glaciated landscape through a
rock-hewn arcaded base and upward in a spiraling tower to a
vast second-floor meeting room. Olmsted has generally been
credited with assisting in the design of the setting, and the

total effect is a superb expression of the Ruskinian sublime in architecture. In Richardson's interpretation, this naturalistic entrance sequence was contained within the overall image of an arcaded European town hall.

The idea of natural growth also appears in Richardson's work in the image of physical growth and decay. Many of his design development drawings show forms such as the tower or the dormer growing out of, or appearing to die back into, other forms in a dynamic process akin to the growth and decay observed in nature. In cases in which a full set of design development drawings has been preserved—for example, those for Austin Hall or the stair tower development for the Glessner house—we can observe Richardson's use of these "organic" design strategies: towers and dormers appear to grow from and fall back into walls and roofs in a playful but dedicated display of design development and testing. Such thinking about nature was key in the design of Memorial Hall, in which Ruskinian and other nineteenth-century ideas about the landscape were united with images of European medieval architecture, such as the raised town hall.

RICHARDSON'S RUSKINIAN PICTURESQUE

Richardson's photograph of himself in a monk's habit is a widely recognized portrait (fig. 1.9). It appears to depict the lighter side of a great man, but the robes were not a Halloween costume. To be sure, the portrait was contrived, yet the image has significant meaning. Richardson displayed it prominently in his office; more important, he sent it to his new clients, such as the Glessners, along with photographs of his major buildings. This image conveys more clearly than words the medieval romanticism that profoundly influenced his genera-

1.9.

H. H. RICHARDSON in monk's habit.
Photo courtesy of the Glessner
House Museum, Chicago.

tion and his entire work.[32] I have distilled this influence as a broad type of design strategy, the "picturesque" in Richardson's work, which I find to be a usual component of other English and American architects who worked in the medieval, Gothic revival, or romantic vocabulary. Ruskin's early architectural writings—particularly *The Seven Lamps of Architecture, The Stones of Venice, Lectures on Architecture and*

Painting, and *Modern Painters*—along with Pugin's earlier influence in a similar direction, contributed to this broad movement in architectural design, stylistically known as the Gothic revival but also evident in many forms of nonclassical or nonformal "Victorian" architecture in the second half of the nineteenth century. I have described this direction in Richardson's work as picturesque despite the term's drawbacks, and I have discussed Memorial Hall at North Easton as a prime example of Richardson's application of the principles of the picturesque. I believe these principles were a driving force behind many of Richardson's finest designs.

Ruskin's early architectural writings helped fuel a revolution in architectural design by providing a rich, multipurpose manifesto for generations of architects practicing in the second half of the nineteenth century and the beginning of the twentieth century. Although Ruskin was not alone in crafting a medievalist, romantic reform message, his long-term influence has surpassed that of all others. Yet today Ruskin's impact is difficult to assess; his vast writings have little appeal for the modern reader, and seventy-five years of relentless modern critique have taken a heavy toll. Furthermore, his incessant moralizing in defense of a challenged Protestant ideology and his unbridled prejudices against the potential benefits of modern architecture and modern life severely compromise his major works. Yet when, for example, Ruskin describes a medieval picturesque building such as St. Mark's, he remains one of the most inspiring architectural enthusiasts who has ever written. We should therefore pay heed to this inspiring Ruskin, who forcefully articulated ideas that, I believe, motivated Richardson to adopt picturesque principles in his many designs.

Notes

1. Contemporaries such as Mariana Griswold Van Rensselaer, *Henry Hobson Richardson and His Works* (1888; facsimile reprint, New York: Dover, 1969), observed many influences in Richardson's work but assumed a Romanesque vocabulary for most projects (86–93). Even early modernist historians, such as Lewis Mumford, saw Richardson as "the last of the great medieval line of master-masons"; *Sticks and Stones: A Study of American Architecture and Civilization,* 2nd rev. ed. (New York: Dover, 1955), 44.

2. Henry-Russell Hitchcock's influential critique is presented in *The Architecture of H. H. Richardson and His Times,* rev. ed. (1961; reprint, Cambridge, Mass.: MIT Press, 1966), 290–303 (1st ed. published in 1936). Hitchcock's negative assessment of most Richardsonian revival buildings has been challenged by more recent scholars, however. For a positive assessment, see *The Spirit of H. H. Richardson on the Midland Prairies: Regional Transformations of an Architectural Style,* ed. Paul Clifford Larson with Susan M. Brown (Minneapolis: University Art Museum, University of Minnesota; Ames: Iowa State University Press, 1988).

3. James F. O'Gorman, *H. H. Richardson: Architectural Forms for an American Society* (Chicago: University of Chicago Press, 1987), 47.

4. As detailed in Thomas C. Hubka, "H. H. Richardson's Glessner House: A Garden in the Machine," *Winterthur Portfolio* 24 (winter 1989): 209–229; and Jeffrey Karl Ochsner and Thomas C. Hubka, "H. H. Richardson: The Design of the William Watts Sherman House," *Journal of the Society of Architectural Historians* 51 (June 1992): 121–145.

5. Hitchcock generally considered the last six years of Richardson's life to be a period of decline, seeing "symptoms of decline" in all but a few of the architect's later works; *Richardson and His Times,* 257. More recently, scholars such as O'Gorman have viewed many buildings of Richardson's final years as ranking among his finest works, *H. H. Richardson,* 47–53.

6. E. H. Gombrich, *Art and Illusion,* 2nd ed. (Princeton: Princeton University Press, 1969), 186–187; Sidney K. Robinson, *Inquiry into the Picturesque* (Chicago: University of Chicago Press, 1991).

7. I cannot cite statistical studies, but I have taught architecture for twenty-five years and I have consistently observed that architectural students across America can expect to hear my colleagues severely criticize a design with "picturesque" characteristics, however the term is defined.

8. Hitchcock generally ignored English medieval and Arts and Crafts influences on Richardson. For example, when writing about the architect's 1882 visit to London, Hitchcock attempts to dismiss his observation of contemporary medieval revival works, his meeting with William Morris, and his visit to William Burges's house (*Richardson and His Times,* 245–246). The contrast to Margaret Henderson Floyd's emphasis on these English influences could not be more striking. See Floyd, *Henry Hobson Richardson: A Genius for Architecture* (New York: Monacelli Press, 1997), 30–65, and passim.

9. Henry-Russell Hitchcock, *Richardson as a Victorian Architect* (Baltimore: published by Smith College at Barton Gillet, 1966); and Hitchcock, "Ruskin and American Architecture, or Regeneration Long Delayed," in *Concerning Architecture: Essays on Architectural Writers and Writing Presented to Nikolaus Pevsner,* ed. John Summerson (London: Allen Lane, 1968), 80–95.

10. Hitchcock, *Richardson and His Times,* 197–199.

11. For a summary, see James F. O'Gorman, *Living Architecture: A Biography of H. H. Richardson* (New York: Simon and Schuster, 1997), 57–73; and Hitchcock, *Richardson and His Times,* 37–50.

12. Hitchcock, *Richardson and His Times,* 129, 197–199.

13. O'Gorman, *Richardson; Architectural Forms,* 29–53.

14. Lyceum Hall, in Winchester, Mass., was designed by Theodore Voelckers, a Boston architect who also designed a town hall for Andover, Mass., in 1858. It, too, included a large second-floor meeting room. Both buildings are illustrated and discussed by Roger G. Reed in "Theodore Voelckers: A Picturesque Public Hall for a New Town," *The Architects of Winchester, Massachusetts,* no. 3 (1996): 5–6 (published by the Winchester Historical Society, ed. Maureen Meister).

15. Examples include the Kaufthaus in Freiburg, Germany, in *European Architecture* 5 (October 1896–October 1897), pl. 509, and the town hall at Arras, France, illustrated in Pierre Lavedan's *Pour*

Connaître les Monuments de France (Paris: Artaud, 1971), pl. 596. Similar civic buildings existed in most European communities from the medieval period into the nineteenth century.

16. Floyd, *Henry Hobson Richardson,* 24–28, 66–86, and 182–191; also my conversations with William H. Pierson, Jr., 1992–1995.

17. Margaret Henderson Floyd, *Architecture after Richardson: Regionalism before Modernism—Longfellow, Alden, and Harlow in Boston and Pittsburgh* (Chicago: University of Chicago Press and the Pittsburgh History and Landmarks Foundation, 1994), 344–345.

18. Everard M. Upjohn, *Richard Upjohn: Architect and Churchman* (New York: Da Capo Press, 1968).

19. Thomas C. Hubka, "Richardson and Ruskin: The Design Principles of H. H. Richardson," paper presented at the Society of Architectural Historians annual meeting, San Francisco, April 1986; and "The Architecture of H. H. Richardson and the Ideas of John Ruskin," paper presented at the Symposium on H. H. Richardson, Forum for American Art, Burchfield Center, N.H., January 1980. Although Richardson does not comment on Ruskin, James F. O'Gorman cites eleven Ruskin books in Richardson's collection in "Documentation: An 1886 Inventory of H. H. Richardson's Library, and Other Gleanings from Probate," *Journal of the Society of Architectural Historians* 41 (May 1982): 150–155.

20. Floyd assumes that a Ruskinian underpinning may be identified in much of Richardson's work. See *Henry Hobson Richardson,* 66–86.

21. Regarding Frank Furness, see George E. Thomas, Michael J. Lewis, and Jeffrey A. Cohen, *Frank Furness: The Complete Works* (New York: Princeton Architectural Press, 1991), 121–165; and on William Burges, see J. Mordaunt Crook, *William Burges and the High Victorian Dream* (Chicago: University of Chicago Press, 1981), 170–252.

22. The failure by any of the major American or European practitioners of Gothic/medieval revival or Arts and Crafts architecture to clearly state design guidelines or principles is a striking contrast to the vast design literature on the classical revival architecture of the same period. A general review of American approaches to nonformal design strategies is given by Mark Mumford, "Form Follows Nature:

The Origins of American Organic Architecture," *Journal of Architectural Education* 42 (spring 1989): 26–37.

23. John Ruskin, "The Lamp of Beauty," chapter 4 of *The Seven Lamps of Architecture* (New York: John Wiley, 1884) (1st ed. published in 1849). Ruskin's general approach to architectural analysis is skillfully analyzed by John Unrau, *Looking at Architecture with Ruskin* (Toronto: University of Toronto Press, 1978). Unrau summarizes Ruskin's integration of architecture, nature, and medieval precedent (13–28, 153–166).

24. Unrau, *Looking at Architecture,* 51–64.

25. Ruskin, *Seven Lamps,* 115.

26. Ibid.

27. Unrau, *Looking at Architecture,* 61–68.

28. H. H. Richardson Collection, Billings and Glessner files, Houghton Library, Harvard University, Cambridge, Mass.

29. Ruskin is quoted in Unrau, *Looking at Architecture,* 62–63.

30. See James D. Kornwolf, "American Architecture and the Aesthetic Movement," in *In Pursuit of Beauty: Americans and the Aesthetic Movement,* by Doreen Bolger Burke et al. (New York: Metropolitan Museum of Art, 1986), 340–383.

31. John Ruskin, *The Stones of Venice* (1851–1853; reprint, Mount Kisco, N.Y.: Moyer Bell Limited, 1989), 74–98.

32. Hubka, "Glessner House," 216–220.

2

INSPIRATION AND SYNTHESIS IN RICHARDSON'S PAINE HOUSE

Margaret Henderson Floyd

H.

H. Richardson's genius was recognized before his death, but the significance of his position in the history of American architecture remains unresolved. Questions persist because his work has long been perceived as unique and relatively isolated from that of his peers. This condition seems less a function of Richardson himself than of the unstudied state of American architectural history of the late nineteenth century from which he emerges.[1] During his lifetime, Richardson's Romanesque style was lauded after the completion of Trinity Church on Boston's Copley Square in 1877; his stature was confirmed as the "Richardsonian Romanesque" spread nationwide. In the years before his death in 1886, Richardson pursued a number of new design directions. In the second quarter of the twentieth century, Henry-Russell Hitchcock exposed and promoted the proto-modern qualities of Richardson's work.[2] More recently, James F. O'Gorman and William H. Pierson, Jr., have explored the relationship between Richardson's buildings and their geological and landscape environments.[3] The character of the American landscape and the impact of Frederick Law Olmsted have been established as generative forces for Richardson.

While drawing on the professional training that he had received in Paris, Richardson worked in a highly personalized Romanesque language, generally understood to have developed through his sensitivity to natural materials and his affinity for the buildings of southern France and Spain. His buildings were marked by three distinguishing attributes that make his work relevant to the development of architecture in the twentieth century: horizontality, visual quiet, and recessive ornament, especially in his later designs; centripetal weight that seemingly imbues the buildings with a geological link to the landscape; and spatial exploitation of the open plan that enhances this environmental sensibility. Yet, with only token connections visible between his work of the 1880s and the "Richardson Romanesque" that initiated his fame, one may still wonder whence these great concepts sprang and how they evolved. Do Parisian method, skill in the Romanesque language, and sensitivity to landscape as promoted by Olmsted adequately explain the sources of Richardson's design innovations? A positive answer to this question appears less defensible as more information emerges about the conditions within which he worked. Richardson responded to various sources of

MARGARET
HENDERSON FLOYD

visual inspiration in the Boston cultural and architectural environment, and he was influenced by his interaction with a significant office staff in the development of his designs. He reacted directly to the architectural stimuli of his day—stimuli that still remain thinly chronicled and poorly understood.

Through an examination of Richardson's Robert Treat Paine house (1883–1886), in Waltham, Massachusetts, as well as a reconsideration of other late works—the Allegheny County Jail, Pittsburgh (1883–1886); the Glessner house, Chicago (1885–1887), the Bigelow house, Newton, Massachusetts (1886–1887), and the railroad stations of the early 1880s—this paper considers some of the conditions and elements of design that connect these structures as a unified body of work. These buildings are fusions of proto-modern ideas with regional visions of New England and with allusions drawn from Norman France and Japan. Richardson subsumed these eclectic sources of inspiration to a broader purpose, synthesizing them to create a transcendent personal statement that endures.

The Robert Treat Paine house, "Stonehurst," in Waltham exhibits an explicit synthesis of duo-colonial, Norman, and Japanese sources (fig. 2.1). Duo-colonial American architectural motifs appear in the dark seventeenth-century shingles and in the overhanging gable with its triple sash, small-paned window, combined with an eighteenth-century Palladian window on the second floor. With these references to colonial American architecture, Richardson has combined two low Norman towers and a recessed loggia on the garden façade. The boulder walls and terrace link the house to the landscape. The cusped gable over the Syrian arch of the east elevation and the projecting dormers above are motifs found in Japanese architecture (fig. 2.2), which was a subject of great interest in

2.1.

H. H. Richardson, Robert Treat
Paine house, Waltham, Mass.,
1883–1886. Photo, ca. 1890s. Courtesy
of the Society for the Preservation of
New England Antiquities, Boston.

———————

Boston at the time the house was completed. Although these motifs had already appeared elsewhere in American domestic design and in other Richardson buildings, Hitchcock, writing in 1936, pronounced: "The Colonial Revival design of the Palladian window in the end gable is as inexplicable as the swooping hood at the northeast corner, which emphasizes the division of the general mass into horizontal layers by the combination of boulder walling below and shingles above."[4]

These eclectic sources presented a problem to Hitchcock, who sought to emphasize Richardson's proto-modern approach to design by portraying him as standing separate from and above his colleagues. The biases of modernism that inspired Hitchcock's work on Richardson, first published sixty years ago, have long since been displaced by a new tolerance of his-

2.2.

"Japanese bazaar," Philadelphia
Centennial Exposition. Lithograph
published by Thomas Hunter, 1876.
Courtesy of the Athenaeum of
Philadelphia.

———————

toric reference in postmodern and contemporary architecture
and criticism. Yet the context of Richardson's practice, which
has been so poorly documented, has only recently started to
yield evidence that he played the game of eclecticism as fully
but more ingeniously than his peers.

In fact, the eclectic elements that Richardson brought
together on the exterior of Stonehurst were also used in the
interior of the house, which, among Richardson's late houses,
stands in unique relationship to the architect. For while
Richardson wrote little and, unlike Louis Sullivan and Frank
Lloyd Wright, left few explications of his work, his design of
his own library attached to his house in Brookline reveals his
personal predilections and the source for details that reappear
in the Paine house. Although contemporary photographs of

·

2.3.

H. H. RICHARDSON, inglenook with
settle benches in the architect's
library, Brookline, Mass., 1880s.
Photo courtesy of the Houghton
Library, Harvard University,
Cambridge, Mass.

this now-destroyed room are black and white, descriptions by two draftsmen in Richardson's office, Albert Elzner and A. W. Longfellow, Jr., cite its terra-cotta red walls decorated with Japanese stencils. The gold-leaf coffers of the beamed ceiling, the elaborate—probably Venetian—wrought-iron light fixture hanging above the desk, and a colonial inglenook with settle benches at the rear of the room (fig. 2.3) all survive in the Paine house, which thus provides a record of Richardson's preferences for his own environment.[5]

Acknowledgment of Richardson's eclectic proclivities allows for straightforward explication of the "inexplicable" exterior of Stonehurst. We know that Richardson's photograph collection contained many images of Normandy around Rouen, that area of France where the architecture is so closely related to that of England. Included in this collection are at least eleven different views of the exterior and interior of the Manoir d'Ango in Varengeville, just south of Dieppe in Normandy.[6] This structure was erected between 1533 and 1545 by Jahan d'Ango, a wealthy armorer who served as mayor of Dieppe. D'Ango, whose name evokes the historical connections between the Normans, Spain, and Naples, played an influential role in the dangerous international politics of the early sixteenth century. Having rescued the kidnapped children of Francis I from imprisonment in Spain by Charles V, d'Ango's royal esteem was, perhaps, unrivaled. The Manoir d'Ango was envisioned as a country retreat for Francis I (and his mistress, Diane de Poitiers). Located seven kilometers south of Dieppe, the Manoir d'Ango was a small château with a large royal block at the south side. The dissimilar towers and arched gateway to the open courtyard were traditional elements in French architecture as were the low towers, which

2.4.

MANOIR D'ANGO, Varengeville,
Normandy, 1533–1545. Photo, 1994, by
William Floyd.

·

MARGARET
HENDERSON FLOYD

appear, for example, in the restorations of Eugène-Emmanuel Viollet-le-Duc at the large château of Pierrefonds or the medieval walled city of Carcassonne. Specific to Dieppe and to the Manoir d'Ango are the Byzantine forms in its design. Modified helmet domes crowned both the tower at the gate and the huge *colombier,* or dovecote, in the center of the courtyard (fig. 2.4). The *colombier* was the largest ever licensed in France and served in the sixteenth century to house the homing pigeons that provided communications to convey intelligence in warfare. The Manoir d'Ango was known in America as a legendary structure by 1901 when Russell Sturgis published his three-volume illustrated *Dictionary of Architecture and Building.*[7]

Interestingly, the impact of the Manoir d'Ango on American architecture in the late nineteenth century has been lost in the shadows of time, not only as an inspiration in the work of Richardson but also in the work of other architects of the period. Richardson appears to have responded to the Manoir d'Ango in the stone towers at the Paine house and at the Albert W. Nickerson house (1886–1887) in Dedham, Massachusetts. Richard Longstreth has noted the close visual relationship between Stanford White's Newport Casino of 1879 and an old photograph of the Manoir d'Ango in White's collection.[8] Restoration of the manoir from its ruinous state began soon after White's trip to France in 1878, when he conversed with the young A. W. Longfellow, Jr., in Paris and probably inspected the manoir. In 1881 Longfellow and Edmund Wheelwright, later the city architect of Boston, visited the site, where they sketched the manoir from the exterior. This visit is documented by Longfellow's drawing published in 1882 on his return to Boston, where he entered Richardson's office.[9] Elements from the manoir would appear in

Longfellow's designs throughout his thirty-year career, and McKim, Mead and White continued to draw on the manoir as a source of inspiration in the Bell house (1880–1881) and others in Newport. The Osborne house and stable of 1885 and the work of many other architects of this period reflect the impact of the Norman châteaux. Wheelwright utilized his own drawings for his designs of the famous Weld estate (now Larz Anderson) carriage house in Brookline of 1887 and, more famously, in the Harvard Lampoon Building in Cambridge of 1909. Though the manoir is lost in the mists of time today, being off the beaten path on which art historians conventionally trace the movement of Renaissance design to Fontainebleau, its role in that development as well as in late-nineteenth-century American architectural history is substantial. The Byzantine character of the helmet dome of the *colombier* and the counterchanged flint and brick of the building's surface appeared repeatedly in American architecture. Also influential were the banded stone of the south exterior wall, which appears in Longfellow's sketch, and more generally the concept of the courtyard house as a whole.

These features of the Manoir d'Ango emerge in the work of Richardson immediately after Longfellow entered the office in the fall of 1881. At the Allegheny County Jail in Pittsburgh, for example, where Longfellow and his future partner Frank Alden were supervising for Richardson, we can look to sources not only in Gridley Bryant's Charles Street Jail, Boston (1852), but also in the manoir. The jail's great wall, running up to the warden's residence, repeats the coursed stonework in Longfellow's sketching vantage as well as the relationship of the entrance and the tower to the flank. At the J. J. Glessner house in Chicago, in addition to the courtyard plan, the original design had a visible external tower. Jeffrey Ochsner's discovery of Longfellow's initials on the presentation plans for the Glessners also connects Longfellow with this commission.[10] We know that Richardson had urged marble, but Glessner's insistence on quarry-faced ashlar prevailed. Longfellow's penchant for the Manoir d'Ango may well have filtered into the executed design of the 18th Street elevation of the house (fig. 2.5), which Shepley, Rutan and Coolidge ultimately produced and which has won such acclaim from historians.

At the Glessner house, other sources of inspiration are revealed. Thomas Hubka has written of Richardson's first designs for the building and has published the staircase, which is described by Glessner as being derived from the staircase of the colonial Vassall-Craigie-Longfellow house in Cambridge, Massachusetts, where A. W. Longfellow was a frequent visitor.[11] Longfellow designed his cousin Alice's modifications to the house and grounds in the years following his uncle's death in 1882. Written records have also revealed that the Glessners met Longfellow on their visit to Boston in the fall of 1885, leaving us to wonder whether they saw the historic house with him but in any case confirming his association with them and their project. Colonial elements such as appear on the Stonehurst exterior were all around Richardson in Boston by 1883.

The magnificent low-lying house for Henry J. Bigelow (fig. 2.6) is an important link in the development of Richardson's late houses. Early plans of the Bigelow house show a courtyard solution, as was used in the urban Glessner house and in the first designs for the Paine house. The unornamented shingled exterior of the Bigelow house draws on the vernacular format for attached New England buildings that Hubka has written of in *Big House, Little House, Back House,*

2.5.

H. H. RICHARDSON, J. J. Glessner
house, Chicago, 1885–1887. Photo, ca.
1960. Courtesy of the Glessner
House Museum, Chicago.

Barn.[12] Sited on a hill with a magnificent view, as were the
Nickerson and Paine houses, the Bigelow house is smaller, with
just one small tower at the corner; but the configuration of the
plan and its relationship to the site are spectacular. The earliest
proposal for Stonehurst was closely related to this house. The
great colonial Palladian window on the east elevation of the
Paine house, with the row of seventeenth-century single-paned
windows and overhang in the changed east gable, mark
Richardson as in midstride of the duo-colonial fashion that was
emerging in the 1880s, when elements from both seventeenth-
and eighteenth-century American architecture were being combined in a single design. These colonial and federal motifs gain

2.6.

H. H. RICHARDSON, Henry J.
Bigelow house, Newton, Mass.,
1886–1887. Photo, 1975. Courtesy of
the Jackson Homestead,
Newton, Mass.

in relevance when one realizes that Richardson's design for Stonehurst is labeled "Mrs. Paine's House." Her inheritance from her father, George Lyman, who lived at the adjacent eighteenth-century Palladian house designed by Samuel McIntire and called the Vale, which Theodore Lyman had built beginning in 1793, allowed the Paines to elevate their house to a more substantial part of the Lyman ancestral holdings in Waltham. The location of this symbol at Mrs. Paine's dressing room, looking toward the Vale, is far from "inexplicable."

The Norman and colonial elements at Stonehurst therefore link Richardson as a designer to both his peers and his clients. But what about the Japanese references at Stonehurst?

It is well known that Richardson's famous Ames Gate Lodge (1880) in North Easton, Massachusetts, and other subsequent work moved from the verticality of the 1870s (characterized by Trinity Church) into a new horizontality. O'Gorman has recognized the influence of the landscape architect Frederick Law Olmsted. Recently, another source has been discovered by Scott Tulay—namely Edward S. Morse, an important figure in the history of Boston architecture.[13] Architectural historians have hitherto overlooked Morse as an influence on Richardson because Morse's book, *Japanese Homes and Their Surroundings*, was not published until 1885, far too late to be associated with either the Ames Gate Lodge or with Richardson's railroad stations—where Japanese forms abound, beginning in 1882 at Auburndale.[14] However, Tulay's research has established that as early as 1878, when Morse returned from Japan with photographs of buildings, he began a series of popular public lectures that culminated ultimately in his Lowell lectures at the Massachusetts Institute of Technology in 1882. For these, Morse used illustrations with both drawings and a magic lantern, beginning at just about the same time that Richardson's style began to change.[15] Morse's lectures received broad coverage in the Boston newspapers after 1882, but local interest in Japan began to be heightened by the lectures in the mid-1870s. Morse's interest in Japan ultimately led to the creation of one of the world's greatest collections of Japanese art at the Museum of Fine Arts. A copy of the first edition of Morse's book (published in late 1885 by the Peabody Museum in Salem) was in Richardson's library.[16]

Yet it is in Richardson's railroad stations, a segment of his work that typologically and historically has been considered somewhat apart, that Tulay's research has exposed the most explicit and direct references to Morse's Japan. The compelling visual correspondence of Richardson's railroad stations to images in Morse's collection of slides and photographs (figs. 2.7 and 2.8) is not surprising in view of other connections between Richardson's office and the Japanese vogue of the day.[17] Morse's book was dedicated to William Sturgis Bigelow, the son of Richardson's client and a leading authority on Japan. Also, Longfellow had been deeply involved with his cousin Charles in designing a Japanese room at the Vassall-Craigie-Longfellow house on Brattle Street in the early 1870s.[18] Charles Longfellow, William Sturgis Bigelow, and Morse paid multiple visits to Japan in this period, traveling together on at least one occasion.

Returning to the changes in the Paine house design, probably in 1885, we see that the yawning Syrian arch of the east elevation is accented with a cusped gable; this curving swelling form, derived from Japanese architecture, had already become a favorite motif in Richardson's work. It appears on the Ames Gate Lodge (see fig. 1.8) as well as on the overhanging dormer that is visible above the east tower. Richardson's use of boulders also may connect his late work with the growing interest in Japan at the time. Although Richardson had used boulders in earlier buildings, beginning with Grace Church in Medford in 1866 and continuing in the structures that he and Olmsted designed for the Fens in Boston, the use of boulders at the Ames Gate Lodge and Stonehurst to link these structures to their sites evokes the stone gardens prevalent in Japan. The terrace with two semicircular ends designed by Olmsted for Stonehurst that lock the house to the landscape lend support to this inference,[19] and a similar form used at the Nickerson house the next year strengthens it further.

2.7.

Country inn in Rikuzen. Drawing
from Edward S. Morse, *Japanese
Homes and Their Surroundings*, 2nd ed.
(Boston: Houghton Mifflin, 1886).

Decoding the Paine house only begins to help us understand Richardson's country house designs and their significance. Looking to Normandy and Japan, Western and Eastern
worlds, and sensitive to burgeoning interests in colonial
American architecture in the wake of the country's centennial,
Richardson did not stand apart from his peers but instead used
the allusions of his time to develop a vision that looked beyond
them. Breaking with the Gothic style in the 1870s when he
adopted Romanesque forms, Richardson in the 1880s produced
the ultimate creative synthesis of eclecticism, projecting his
age to the next.

2.8.

H. H. RICHARDSON, Boston and
Albany Railroad Station, Brighton,
Mass., 1884–1885. Photo. Courtesy of
the Houghton Library, Harvard
University.

Notes

During the months before her death on 18 October 1997, Margaret
Henderson Floyd outlined her thoughts for revising this essay. She
was planning to expand it considerably and had given it the working
title "Decoding the Country House Designs." She also was completing a manuscript for a book on Richardson, *H. H. Richardson: A
Genius for Architecture*, published at the end of 1997, whose final chapter examined the architect's country houses. She still had more to say
about the topic, and she looked forward to developing those ideas further for this publication; but she died before she could realize those
plans. The essay published here is, with minor editing, the paper that
she delivered at North Easton in 1996. This essay, therefore, repre-
sents a point of departure for ideas that she reworked in her book on
Richardson. At the same time, it offers a concentrated study, seen

·

INSPIRATION AND

SYNTHESIS

through the prism of the Robert Treat Paine house, of Floyd's under-standing of Richardson's buildings, his fellow architects, and the context in which Boston architects worked during the late nineteenth century—concerns that she explored throughout her scholarly career.

Notes and illustrations have been added by the editor.

1. For further study of Margaret Henderson Floyd's writings on late-nineteenth-century American architecture, see the following: *Architectural Education and Boston,* centennial publication of the Boston Architectural Center (Boston: Boston Architectural Center, 1989); *Architecture after Richardson: Regionalism before Modernism—Longfellow, Alden, and Harlow in Boston and Pittsburgh* (Chicago: University of Chicago Press and the Pittsburgh History and Landmarks Foundation, 1994); and *Henry Hobson Richardson: A Genius for Architecture* (New York: Monacelli Press, 1997).

2. Henry-Russell Hitchcock, *The Architecture of H. H. Richardson and His Times,* rev. ed. (Hamden, Conn.: Archon Books, 1961) (1st ed. published in 1936).

3. James F. O'Gorman, *H. H. Richardson: Architectural Forms for an American Society* (Chicago: University of Chicago Press, 1987); William H. Pierson, Jr., in *Macmillan Encyclopedia of Architects,* ed. Adolf K. Placzek (New York: Free Press, 1982), s.v. "H. H. Richardson."

4. Hitchcock, *Richardson and His Times,* 269.

5. For further discussion of Richardson's library, see James F. O'Gorman, *H. H. Richardson and His Office: A Centennial of His Move to Boston, 1874: Selected Drawings* (Cambridge, Mass.: Department of Printing and Graphic Arts, Harvard College Library, 1974), 4–13.

6. Photographs of the Manoir d'Ango from Richardson's collection are reproduced in Floyd, *Henry Hobson Richardson,* 26, figs. 16, 17, and 18.

7. Russell Sturgis, ed., *A Dictionary of Architecture and Building: Biographical, Historical, and Descriptive,* 3 vols. (New York: Macmillan, 1901–1902), s.v. "Renaissance Architecture," fig. 2.

8. Richard Longstreth, "Academic Eclecticism in American Architecture," *Winterthur Portfolio* 17 (spring 1982): 55–82.

9. Longfellow's drawing appears in Floyd, *Henry Hobson Richardson*, 121, fig. 118.

10. Jeffrey Ochsner told the author about the appearance of Longfellow's initials on the plans in April 1994. The plans are dated "5/85," indicating that they were drawn in May of 1885.

11. Thomas C. Hubka, "H. H. Richardson's Glessner House: A Garden in the Machine," *Winterthur Portfolio* 24 (winter 1989): 209–229.

12. Thomas C. Hubka, *Big House, Little House, Back House, Barn: The Connected Farm Buildings of New England* (Hanover, N.H.: University Press of New England, 1984).

13. Scott Tulay, "Edward S. Morse and Japanese Architecture: Inspiration for H. H. Richardson in the 1880s" (senior honors thesis, Tufts University, 1992).

14. Edward S. Morse, *Japanese Homes and Their Surroundings,* 2nd ed. (1886; reprint, New York: Dover, 1961) (1st ed. published in 1885).

15. Edward S. Morse Archives, Peabody Essex Museum, Salem, Mass.

16. James F. O'Gorman, "Documentation: An 1886 Inventory of H. H. Richardson's Library, and Other Gleanings from Probate," *Journal of the Society of Architectural Historians* 41 (May 1982): 150–155.

17. For additional comparisons between Richardson's railroad stations and Japanese architecture, see Floyd, *Henry Hobson Richardson,* 192–201.

18. Nancy K. Jones, "The Crossover of Japanese Decorative Arts into Architecture: The Charles Longfellow Japan Room of 1874" (seminar report, Tufts University, December 1996).

19. On the interaction between Richardson and Olmsted at Stonehurst, see Margaret Henderson Floyd, "H. H. Richardson, Frederick Law Olmsted, and the House for Robert Treat Paine," *Winterthur Portfolio* 18 (winter 1983): 227–248.

3

THE VEIL OF NATURE: H. H. Richardson and Frederick Law Olmsted

Francis R. Kowsky

I n 1865, when Henry Hobson Richardson settled in New York after several years of study and work in Paris, Central Park ranked as one of the newest attractions of the city (fig. 3.1). Also in that year, Calvert Vaux, the park's co-designer with Frederick Law Olmsted, with much cajoling convinced Olmsted to return to New York from California, where he had gone to seek his fortune as manager of the Mariposa Mining Company. The two men resumed their partnership and started work on Prospect Park in Brooklyn. Over the next several years, they went on to create other parks in many American cities. During this period, young Richardson, a fledgling member of New York's architectural profession, came to know Olmsted and

3.1.

CALVERT VAUX, Ramble Arch,

Central Park, New York City, 1859.

Photo from Samuel Parsons, Jr.,

Landscape Gardening (New York,

1891).

Vaux. All three men shared an interest in promoting the new American Institute of Architects. The three also held membership in the Century, an elite club of artists, architects, and men of letters.

At the Century and at AIA meetings, which sometimes took place in Vaux's office, Richardson would have heard discussions of issues vital to the art life of the city. One wonders what he, fresh from Paris, must have thought about the controversy that had developed in 1863 over the gates that Richard Morris Hunt, Richardson's American predecessor at the Ecole des Beaux-Arts, had proposed for the 59th Street entrances to Central Park. Surely Olmsted, and possibly Vaux, would have told Richardson how such grandiose classical imagery thwarted the romantic spirit of the Greensward design (the name they gave their 1858 successful entry in the park design competition). Vaux, who had borne the brunt of the battle to save the park from these intrusions, would have repeated to Richardson his dislike of the formal tradition of French garden design that Hunt's gates represented and that Vaux unfavorably identified with the antidemocratic rule of Napoleon III. This objection to Hunt's design may well have been the first time that Richardson was made aware of the moral bias held by Olmsted and Vaux against the Renaissance conception of landscape art that Richardson would have absorbed as part of his Parisian training.

Olmsted and Richardson, fellow residents of Staten Island, became friends. Olmsted, fifteen years Richardson's senior and well known in certain circles of New York's cultural elite, could have piloted the younger man through the unfamiliar milieu of his newly adopted city. The two men also seemed to complement each other personally. To Richardson's expansive disposition and love of good food and stimulating talk, Olmsted brought a political philosopher's concern with social issues and a workaholic's devotion to detail. Vaux had nicknamed him "Frederick the Great" for his preoccupation with controlling and managing park work crews and policemen. And one wonders what Olmsted—whom Vaux once admonished to treat his wife to a new dress—must have thought of the profligacy Richardson displayed on the evening of moving into his new Staten Island home when he lit roaring fires in all the fireplaces. Differences of temperament aside, Richardson and Olmsted shared a certain slant of mind, and gradually they developed a strong attachment to each other. After Richardson's death, it fell to Olmsted to try to straighten out his friend's tangled, debt-ridden affairs.

During the late 1860s, Richardson and Olmsted began to collaborate professionally. The Staten Island Improvement Plan and the memorial for Alexander Bache in Washington's Congressional Cemetery were tentative beginnings to what would become a celebrated relationship in American architecture. But Olmsted never formed a contractual partnership with Richardson as he had done with Vaux. Unlike Andrew Jackson Downing, America's earliest proponent of the romantic school of landscape architecture, Olmsted saw no advantage in allying himself with an architect. Indeed, from a working standpoint, he found many things unsatisfactory about his alliance with Vaux's architectural practice, which included the architect Frederick Clarke Withers. Despite being associated professionally with Vaux and Withers, in 1868 Olmsted probably recommended to William Dorsheimer that he hire Richardson to design his new house on Delaware Avenue in Buffalo. It was the architect's first important dwelling. At the time, Olmsted was leading his firm's efforts to formulate a park and parkway system for Buffalo. Dorsheimer, the local district attorney, was a prime mover in that endeavor.

Two years later, Richardson received a commission in Buffalo that was far more important for the future of his art.[1] The Buffalo State Hospital (1870; fig. 3.2), today Buffalo Psychiatric Center, was the architect's first big job. With this

3.2.

H. H. RICHARDSON, Buffalo State
Hospital (now Buffalo Psychiatric
Center), Buffalo, N.Y., 1870.
FREDERICK LAW OLMSTED, Buffalo
State Hospital grounds, 1876.
Photo by author.

building, he ventured to inform his architecture with his own robust temperament and invented the rugged medievalist style that became synonymous with his name. At the Buffalo State Hospital, Richardson also learned how Olmsted and Vaux approached the problem of planning a building in relation to its site. As the landscape architects to the project, Olmsted and Vaux determined the unusual alignment of the extended group of pavilions. Instead of paralleling the street, the birds-in-flight configuration of central administration building and flanking patients' wards inclined toward the southeast. The angle allowed the patients to enjoy maximum sunlight during the winter months. (It is tempting to believe that Richardson's experience at the Buffalo State Hospital influenced his decision several years later to align the spaces of his Winn Memorial Library [1876–1879] in Woburn, Massachusetts, along an axis that provided the building's interior with the greatest amount of natural light.) In 1876, Olmsted prepared a landscape plan for the hospital grounds; it was his first experience with creating a setting for one of Richardson's buildings. Olmsted's scheme included a curving approach road bordered with thickly planted hedges and tall shrubs and a parklike area in front of the hospital where patients might enjoy the out-of-doors in tranquil surroundings. Some of this landscape plan survives today. In effect, Olmsted transformed the windswept asylum acreage into a pastoral landscape of lawns, trees, walks, and drives similar to that he had created in the Park, the major greenspace of the new Buffalo park and parkway system that lay adjacent to the institution's property.

The year 1872 marked a turning point in the careers of both Richardson and Olmsted. Richardson won the competition for Boston's Trinity Church. Also in 1872, for various reasons, Olmsted and Vaux decided to end their partnership, although they were to remain friends for the rest of their lives. Furthermore, Olmsted was becoming weary of New York. Ignorant park commissioners and meddling politicians were confounding his and Vaux's efforts to maintain and extend the ideals embodied in their Greensward plan. In 1881, Olmsted moved permanently to the Boston suburb of Brookline, the wealthiest town in America, where he again became a neighbor of Richardson, now his close friend.

During the last few years of his life, Richardson designed suburban houses, libraries, and other projects for which Olmsted directed the layout of the grounds. At least once in these later years, Olmsted counseled Richardson to go to Central Park to refresh his memory of archways and other structures constructed there by Vaux in the 1860s. We have no record of any such visit, but Richardson was frequently in the city and could easily have acted on his friend's advice. We also can assume that Olmsted often discussed with Richardson the philosophy behind the design of those structures: making them appear secondary to the surrounding landscape. I believe that one can see a reflection of Central Park's rusticated stone arches in the ground-hugging cyclopean arch of the Ames Gate Lodge.[2] It straddles the road leading into the property and frames the visitor's view of the landscape beyond in the way that Vaux's archways do in Central Park. Also, like the exterior of those park structures, the rocks of the gate lodge (and other country buildings by Richardson) would have grown a lush mantel of ivy to merge them more completely with their surroundings. And sometime Olmsted must have taken Richardson on either an actual or verbal stroll through Central Park's picturesque Ramble to the Belvedere. The

3.3.

H. H. RICHARDSON with FREDERICK
LAW OLMSTED, Oakes Ames
Memorial Hall, North Easton,
Mass., 1879–1881. Photo from H. H.
Richardson, *The Ames Memorial
Buildings, North Easton, Mass.,*
Monographs of American
Architecture, 3 (Boston: Ticknor,
1886).

placement of that structure atop a large rock outcropping with a pathway approaching it among boulders seems to anticipate the siting of Oakes Ames Memorial Hall (1879–1881) on its craggy hilltop in North Easton, Massachusetts (fig. 3.3).

Harmony between building and setting especially informs the suburban railroad stations that Richardson designed and Olmsted landscaped. Planned between 1881 and 1885 for the pleasure and convenience of Boston commuters, most of these stations were located along the main line of the Boston and Albany Railroad, whose board of directors included friends of both Richardson and Olmsted.[3] That railway also encompassed a three-mile tributary that the board created in 1883 and called the Newton Circuit. Richardson's railroad station designs were intimate in scale and generous in proportion and materials. They also formed, in the words of Margaret Henderson Floyd, "the earliest sustained application of Japanese inspiration in American architecture."[4] The stations must have seemed remarkably humane to those who first used them. Olmsted sought to complement Richardson's quiet, reassuring architecture with plants, mostly native New England species, arranged in informal ways. At times, he added boulders to the landscape, as if to recall the primeval link that existed between the rusticated stones of the station walls and the earth from which they came.

According to Charles Mulford Robinson, the aesthetically astute writer and city planner who, at the turn of the century, championed the stations that Richardson and Olmsted's collaboration produced, the impetus behind the creation of a "railroad beautiful" could be traced to the example of a local stationmaster. The employee's personal attempts to embellish the station at Newtonville with flowers and plants drew the attention of Charles Sprague Sargent, the director of the Arnold Arboretum and a Boston and Albany director. Sargent suggested to his fellow board members that they might attract more city dwellers to the suburbs if all of the company's stations were tastefully landscaped. With Richardson already providing station designs, the moment appeared right to act. Olmsted, a friend of Sargent, was hired to do the job.[5] (In addition, a grateful board elevated the enterprising stationmaster, whose name was also Richardson, to superintendent of all station grounds.) Under Olmsted's direction, the railroad set up its own nurseries to stock hardy shrubs, trees, and border plants that could survive the harsh conditions encountered at the stations. Notably absent from Olmsted's plans were the showy displays of flowers that the public often associated with railroad station yards. Just as he and Vaux had done in their large public parks, Olmsted employed a subtle green palette of evergreen and deciduous shrubs and trees and herbaceous plants, often densely grouped, to enhance the year-round allure of the stations and to conceal nearby utilitarian structures. In color, texture, and arrangement, his range complemented perfectly Richardson's compact and unaffected architectural expression.

In the early spring of 1884, Olmsted wrote to Frederick L. Ames with instructions for planting the grounds around the Old Colony station (a line that also sought Richardson and Olmsted's services) at North Easton.[6] Olmsted's desire for *Plantanus* and *gleditscha* [sic] would not be easily met, but Ames assured the designer that he had plenty of hemlocks, birches, and junipers on hand in his nursery. He merely waited for Olmsted to come to the site and set out stakes where workmen were to transplant the trees. Ames also expected Olmsted

to indicate where he wanted to locate a large boulder that he
wished to stand among a clump of hemlocks and birches. And
as on park structures, creepers were to be trained across the station's rough granite walls. There is no reason to doubt that the
great architect warmly endorsed his friend's ideas and would
have seconded James O'Gorman's statement that the depot
"acted as an intermediary between the railroad tracks leading
away from the country and the view of the woods, meadows,
and waterways of the Ames estate landscaped by Olmsted."[7]
Just as he had done with Vaux, Olmsted came to share with
Richardson a vision of architecture in harmony with nature,

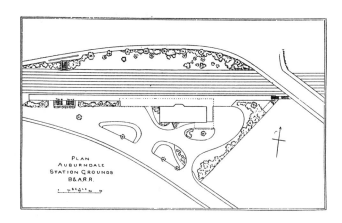

3.5.

FREDERICK LAW OLMSTED, Boston
and Albany Railroad Station,
Auburndale, Mass., 1881, plan of
grounds. From *Garden and Forest* 2 (13
March 1889).

although Richardson experienced the plantings around his stations only as saplings.

In their imaginations, Richardson and Olmsted must have envisioned their Boston and Albany stations as they are shown in early twentieth-century photographs—nestled into their surroundings like the park structures around which Olmsted and Vaux had drawn the veil of nature. At much-altered Wellesley Hills (1885–1886; fig. 3.4), we are told, Olmsted used copious vegetation to heal the unsightly cut of the trackbed that railroad engineers had made through the countryside. "Ledges and retaining walls were adorned with climbing plants and vines that produced a natural impression," wrote J. H. Phillips, an early admirer of Richardson and Olmsted's stations.[8] Olmsted was also mindful of the genius of the place and preserved and enhanced interesting nearby topographic features. The pond adjacent to the Wellesley Hills station was brought to life with many aquatic plants, and the little pool at Woodland was embellished with dense border vegetation.

The Auburndale station, which Richardson designed in 1881 for Newton, was the first stop to benefit from Olmsted's efforts (fig. 3.5). After the station was completed, Olmsted laid out the approach drive and pedestrian walks and planned the vegetation.[9] Shrubs ornamented the small traffic islands and screened the surroundings from view, and woodbine and Virginia creeper draped the granite station walls (fig. 3.6). To accentuate the idea of shelter conveyed by the long sweeping lines of the roof and porch of Richardson's building, Olmsted placed a single elm tree next to the porte cochere (fig. 3.7). Beneath its developed overarching branches, women passengers entered and left the waiting room provided especially for them. Across from the outdoor trackside platform, Olmsted put in the ground a variety of bushes (especially lilacs) to hide the fence that bordered the company property on the other side of the tracks—just as he and Vaux had planted out the city around Central Park with a high wall of trees and shrubs. In this way, Olmsted gave the tarrying commuter what the journal *Garden and Forest* called "a pleasant, verdurous prospect whichever way he [might] turn his eyes."[10] Furthermore, a subterranean passage allowed pedestrians from the opposite side of the tracks to approach or leave the now-vanished Auburndale station without the trains causing danger or delay. This provision recalled the practice of "separation of ways" that Olmsted and Vaux initiated in Central Park; there, by means of archways, pedestrian paths went either over or under their

3.6.

H. H. Richardson with Frederick
Law Olmsted, Boston and Albany
Railroad Station, Auburndale.
Drawing from *Garden and Forest* 2 (13
March 1889).

---

intersection with carriage drives and bridle paths. Like
Olmsted and Vaux's urban parks, the Boston and Albany station grounds showed in their designs as much concern for people's safety and convenience as for their enjoyment of natural
beauty.

All of these ideas were present at the Chestnut Hill station
(sadly, also demolished; 1883–1884), which Richardson and
Olmsted's contemporaries regarded as their finest effort to
treat the modern railroad station artistically (fig. 3.8). Like
Olmsted and Vaux's parks, the granite-and-brownstone station
and its leafy grounds stood apart from the life of the town in
fictive rural retirement. From the street, one went to meet the
train, reported Charles Robinson, following "roads and paths
winding luxuriously down to the little station building."[11]

3.7.

H. H. Richardson with Frederick
Law Olmsted, Boston and Albany
Railroad Station, Auburndale. Photo
from *Garden and Forest* 2 (13 March
1889).

———————————

Pedestrians taking the staircase from the street especially
enjoyed a walk through "a natural arch of bush and tree" on
their way to the porte cochere. Together with the willow-
shaded lawn, the building and shrubbery created a picture so
compelling that Robinson could imagine "a businessman
choosing Chestnut Hill for his place of residence for no other
reason than the soothing charm with which its little station
would daily wait his return and the lingering caress of beauty
with which it would send him forth."[12]

In their day, these delightful suburban spaces, with their
curving walks and drives, were compared to parks and gardens.
"Veritable gateways of rural beauty," Phillips called them, and
Mariana Van Rensselaer commented on how pleasant it was for
her to while away an hour in their tasteful seclusion.[13] From

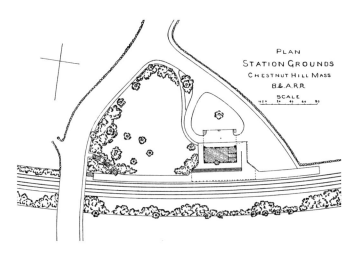

3.8.

FREDERICK LAW OLMSTED, Boston
and Albany Railroad Station,
Chestnut Hill (Newton), Mass., 1884,
plan of grounds. From *Garden and
Forest* 2 (3 April 1889).

time to time, the clattering engines of which Richardson was
so fond would disturb the serenity of these verdant cottage
grounds of ivy-covered walls, lush lawns, and thick hedges.
Icons of stasis and dynamism, of the soft-edged world of home
and the hard-edged world of the rushing city, the stations and
the railroad proclaimed the nineteenth century's desire to wed
the garden with the machine. This desire was especially evident in the landscape and stations along the Newton Circuit,
which had the character of a linear park whose stations were
incidental to the general scenic effect. Begun in 1883, the
Newton Circuit may have had the advantage of Richardson
and Olmsted's advice on how to design the trackbed and site
the stations, even before construction was undertaken.

(Richardson's depots at Eliot, Woodland, and Waban were commissioned in 1884.) "The day I made the round of the stations" on the Newton Circuit, reported Robinson in 1902, "the air was sweet with the perfume of wild roses which, in orderly disorder, climbed the banks on either side." And all along the way, little evidence of human structures intruded on his view. "The very telegraph poles were so hidden in the shrubbery that they were scarcely noticeable," he said. Both Robinson's descriptions and historic photographs attest that the rail line and Richardson and Olmsted's stations celebrated in living form what Leo Marx calls that "evocative juxtaposition of the mechanical artifact with the shapes, lines, colors, and textures of the natural setting" that fascinated the romantic age.[14]

Writing to his friend Charles Eliot Norton, Olmsted expressed the opinion that true art education should teach people to comprehend the beauty of the natural world. They would then be able, as he was, to love the colors of a rain-soaked landscape or the jewel-like glow of a late evening sky, or feel an exhilarating sense of freedom when they gazed at a wide expanse of meadow dotted with groves of stately trees—a greensward.[15] To Van Rensselaer, Olmsted recounted how, in 1875, he acted as teacher and guide to his friend Richardson at Niagara Falls, instructing him in the distinctive charms of its matchless physical setting. Olmsted explained to Richardson how the cataract represented only a portion of the special beauty of shoreline, rapids, and woods that one could experience there. Richardson willingly let himself be led by his eloquent and sensitive friend along now-vanished paths through dense woods and groves, remembered today only in pictures. At Niagara, Olmsted, who a decade later would collaborate with Vaux to plan a park there, related how Richardson placed himself completely in Olmsted's hands for a tour of the area. "This is a matter in which you are an expert," the architect assured his friend in a spirit of good-natured irony, "and I will not take off the least share of your responsibility." Over the course of a long afternoon, Olmsted guided Richardson around Goat Island. With the sound of the great river blending with his words, Olmsted would have shown his guest many spots from which one could enjoy vignettes of forest and water scenery. Olmsted himself found that watching the onrushing waters of the rapids above the falls produced a more agreeable sensation than viewing the falls themselves. Throughout the day, Richardson, like an obedient pupil, suppressed his impatience to see the falls and entered fully into Olmsted's enthusiasm for the exceptional beauty of the less awesome aspects of the famous site. Indeed, it was only on the second day of their visit, Olmsted says, that he took Richardson to the brink of the cataract. Enlightened by the experience of the previous afternoon, the normally ebullient Richardson avoided "amazement, and was willing to sit for hours in one place, contemplatively enjoying the beauty."[16] This is a touching record of Olmsted mentoring Richardson in the thoughtful appreciation of natural scenery. Olmsted had won a convert to his and Vaux's way of seeing.

In general, Olmsted found architects unsympathetic or insensitive to nature. He complained that they either thought of their buildings in isolation from the natural environment or intended to make them the dominant feature of a landscape.[17] Since the early days of Central Park, Olmsted had called for just the opposite approach, asking architects of rural, suburban, and park buildings to think first of how their design might rest in its God-given setting. Surely Olmsted instructed

Richardson many times in this philosophy, which had earlier guided Vaux in the dwellings he had built along the Hudson and in his designs for bridges in Central Park. In one of his characteristically expansive moods, Richardson prodded Olmsted to construct a new house, which he cheerfully proposed to design for a lot behind his own home in Brookline. "A beautiful thing in shingles" Richardson vowed it would be.[18] And in a sketch he showed his friend how a new drive could be laid out to accommodate the dwelling. Like the buildings in Olmsted and Vaux's parks, it would be nicely tucked away from view. Although Olmsted seems never to have seriously considered building the house, he must have appreciated Richardson's grasp of his notion of studied informality.

Yet he and Vaux were to see that conception gravely threatened after Richardson's death, when a new wave of classicism in landscape architecture accompanied the rise of neoclassicism in the building arts. Olmsted raged against Stanford White, Richard Morris Hunt, and others like them as "doctrinaires and fanatics and essentially cockneys, with no more knowledge of nor interest in real rurality than most men of Parisian training and associations."[19] One of those men of Parisian training whom he had nevertheless succeeded in converting to what might be called the "Greensward aesthetic" was his late friend H. H. Richardson.

Notes

1. I discuss this project in "Architecture, Nature and Humanitarian Reform: The Buffalo State Hospital for the Insane," in *Changing Places: Remaking Institutional Buildings,* ed. Lynda H. Schneekloth, Marcia F. Feuerstein, and Barbara A. Campagna (Fredonia, N.Y.: White Pine Press, 1992), 43–63.

2. I explore the relation between Richardson's gate lodge and Vaux's bridges in "H. H. Richardson's Ames Gate Lodge and the Romantic Landscape Tradition," *Journal of the Society of Architectural Historians* 50 (June 1991): 181–188.

3. For the history of these stations, see Jeffrey Karl Ochsner, "Architecture for the Boston and Albany Railroad, 1881–1894," *Journal of the Society of Architectural Historians* 47 (June 1988): 109–131.

4. Margaret Henderson Floyd, *Henry Hobson Richardson: A Genius for Architecture* (New York: Monacelli Press, 1997), 200.

5. C. M. Robinson, "A Railroad Beautiful," *House and Garden* 2 (November 1902): 564.

6. Olmsted's letter is lost, but its content can be surmised from Frederick L. Ames's reply dated 29 April 1884 in the Frederick Law Olmsted Papers, Manuscript Division, Library of Congress, Washington, D.C.

7. James F. O'Gorman, *Living Architecture: A Biography of H. H. Richardson* (New York: Simon and Schuster, 1997), 131.

8. J. H. Phillips, "The Evolution of the Suburban Station," *Architectural Record* 36 (August 1914): 125. The Wellesley Hills station was commissioned from Richardson in 1885 and landscaped after its completion in January 1886.

9. Olmsted's plan, which is preserved at the Olmsted National Historic Site, Brookline, Mass., is dated 3 May 1882.

10. "The Railroad Station at Auburndale, Massachusetts," *Garden and Forest* 2 (13 March 1889): 125.

11. Robinson, "A House Beautiful," 569.

12. Ibid. Olmsted's plan for Chestnut Hill station, dated 9 February 1884, is at the Olmsted National Historic Site, Brookline, Mass.

13. Phillips, "Evolution," and Mariana Griswold Van Rensselaer, *Henry Hobson Richardson and His Works* (Boston: Houghton Mifflin, 1888), 102.

14. Leo Marx, "The Railroad-in-the-Landscape: An Iconological Reading of a Theme in American Art," in *The Railroad in American Art: Representation of Technological Change,* ed. Susan Danly and Leo Marx (Cambridge, Mass.: MIT Press, 1988), 183.

15. Frederick Law Olmsted to Charles Eliot Norton, 22 January 1880. Frederick Law Olmsted Papers.

16. Olmsted is quoted in Van Rensselaer, *Henry Hobson Richardson,* 27.

17. See especially Olmsted's "Lecture to Students of Architecture," typescript, ca. 1892. Frederick Law Olmsted Papers

18. Henry Hobson Richardson to Frederick Law Olmsted, 6 February 1883. Frederick Law Olmsted Papers.

19. Frederick Law Olmsted to William Stiles, 10 March 1895. Frederick Law Olmsted Papers.

4

THEN AND NOW: A Note on the Contrasting Architectures of H. H. Richardson and Frank Furness

James F. O'Gorman

I read my first book of architectural history over
forty-five years ago. It was the required text in
Lawrence Hill's survey at Washington University in
St. Louis: Sir Banister Fletcher's *History of
Architecture on the Comparative Method* of 1896. Then
in its fifteenth edition (and currently in its eighteenth, with its
title shortened to avoid any distasteful reference to its "dated"
method), this classic is a century old. Much printer's ink has
spilled over the methodological dam since the *History* first
appeared, but I here and now come out of the closet, show
myself to be an unredeemed mossback, and adapt Sir Banister's
nineteenth-century comparative approach for my final contribution to the study of H. H. Richardson's work. I think we can

learn much about the character of his architectural achievement by silhouetting it against that of one of his peers, Philadelphia's Frank Furness.

Richardson (1838–1886) and Furness (1839–1912) were almost exact contemporaries who shared an Anglo-Saxon and Unitarian heritage, somewhat common professional educational experiences, and the eclectic design propensities of their age.[1] They certainly knew one another's work, if not one another. They were poles apart in place of birth and preferred residence, in appearance and personality, in their experiences during the Civil War, and—as we will see—in the very different clienteles they served in very different urban centers.[2] At the top of the professional food chain, they represented in gilt-aged America two diametrically opposed architectural agendas. A discussion of both tells much about each, and for our present purpose, the comparison somewhat alters the customary reading of Richardson's historical position—and therefore his legacy.

Since the modernist apologies of Henry-Russell Hitchcock and others, Richardson has been viewed as a proto-modernist, a precursor of the self-styled ahistorical works of the mid-twentieth century. Critics have approached my own writings on the architect with just such a bias, assuming that my placing him first in a line of succession to Sullivan and Wright meant that I endorsed his putative position as progenitor of "progressive" modernism. In fact I see the works of all three architects as *of* rather than *ahead* of their times; that is, as based on the possibilities of the historical moment in which they were created rather than reaching for something beyond contemporary potential.[3] As this glance at the work of a coexistent architect will show, Richardson's output was antimodern even in reference to his own time rather than proto-modern in reference to a later date.

In a paper as brief as this, I can only suggest rather than prove. I will make my point by Banisterian comparative observations about selected pairs of buildings by Richardson and Furness that are as close in time and in program as conditions permit, then add some observations about the different clienteles the architects served. Each might be said to have "arrived" professionally in the early 1870s: Richardson (in partnership with Charles Gambrill, who had been Furness's mate in Richard Morris Hunt's atelier in the 1850s) with his winning design for Trinity Church (1872–1877) in Boston, and Furness (in partnership with George Hewitt) with the winning design for the Pennsylvania Academy of the Fine Arts (1871–1876) in Philadelphia. The contrast between the two buildings is striking, certainly in part because the programs were different—a church on the one hand and a museum and school on the other—but in part, too, because of differing design intentions. And this difference goes beyond Richardson's choice of Romanesque arches and Furness's choice of Gothic.

Both architects looked to past forms, but each rendered them in a different way. Richardson employed load-bearing wood and masonry in a structure whose ancestry may be traced through Stonehenge to the origins of architecture. Furness's structural system is also traditional, but it is realized in materials and techniques developed in the course of the nineteenth century. And the contrast embodies more than the differences in structural materials; it affects architectural form as well. Trinity appears to be Romanesque Revival, period; the Academy mingles French Second Empire, Venetian Gothic, and Islamic accents with forms generated by the latest technology.

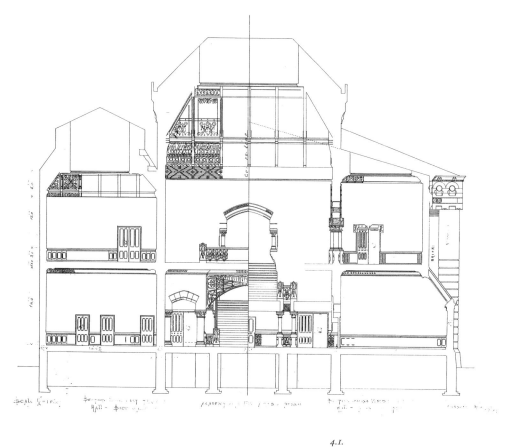

4.1.

FURNESS AND HEWITT, the
Pennsylvania Academy of the Fine
Arts, Philadelphia, 1871–1876.
Transverse section looking west
(preliminary design). Courtesy of the
Pennsylvania Academy of the Fine
Arts, Philadelphia.

4.2.

FURNESS AND HEWITT, the
Pennsylvania Academy. North
elevation. Author's collection.

A transverse section through the Academy (fig. 4.1) reveals on the lower right a dramatic—even daring—use of structural iron to admit north light into the studios at ground level. The skylight is a glass shed angling upward from the top of the ground-level masonry wall to the lowest chord of an iron truss. From within the studio, the massive bolts securing the tension members of the truss are exposed, and the iron beams and brick arches supporting the floor of the museum above are visible as well. On the exterior, the Cherry Street elevation presents a characteristic Furnessic chaos of visual parts (fig. 4.2). Among them an exposed metallic truss supports the wall

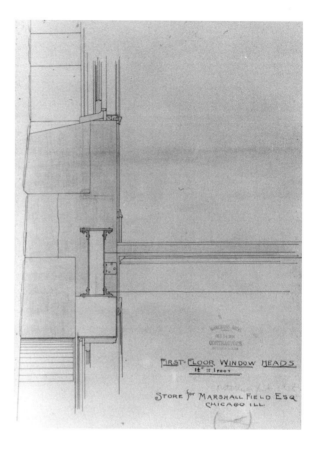

4.3.

H. H. RICHARDSON, Marshall Field
Wholesale Store, Chicago, 1885–1887.
Section through first-floor window
heads. Courtesy of the Houghton
Library, Harvard University,
Cambridge, Mass.

4.4.

H. H. RICHARDSON, Field store.
Detail of exterior. Photo. Courtesy of
the Chicago Historical Society.

above the continuous skylight, a wall whose brick patterns echo the triangles of the truss. Furness thus makes architectural coin out of engineering necessity.[4]

You might say that visible engineering forms were appropriate for the lower and private artists' studios at the Academy, but Furness also exposed iron beams in the upstairs public exhibition galleries and supported them with iron posts that incorporated the forced-air heating system as well. There is little at Trinity—or in any of Richardson's buildings—to parallel Furness's architectural use of these characteristic nineteenth-century features. When, for example, Richardson exposed iron posts in a window at the Brattle Square Church (1869–1873) in Boston, that window looked out on a narrow alley, and that use of iron had no impact on the interior spatial effect. When, again, Richardson showed the bolt securing the tension rod that supports the midpoint of the main—wooden—beam above the living hall at the Robert Treat Paine house (1883–1886) in Waltham, Massachusetts, he embellished it with a hammered-iron, artsy-crafty cartouche. No raw engineering details for him.

Or contrast the section through the north wall of the Pennsylvania Academy with that through the main façades of Richardson's later Marshall Field Wholesale Store (1885–1887) in Chicago (fig. 4.3). The spatial manipulation achieved in the one by means of the bare metallic structure is absent in the other. Richardson's section shows a massive masonry wall within which is hidden an iron box girder spanning the heads of the ground-floor openings. Hidden, that is, so that the architectural expression of the façade will recall the Pont-du-Gard at Nîmes or the Palazzo Pitti in Florence, both traditional load-bearing masonry systems (fig. 4.4). (That this drawing might actually stem from the office of his builder, Norcross Brothers, in no way alters the point. Architect and builder were hand-in-glove collaborators.) Richardson might on occasion seek the structural aid of the new industrial materials, but he would not give them an architectural task.

Frederick Law Olmsted dictated the use of iron plate girders in the railroad bridge in Boston's Fenway (1880–1883). The exposed iron girders in the courtrooms at the Allegheny County buildings (1883–1888) in Pittsburgh were put in place after Richardson's death.[5] More characteristic of his architectural proclivities is the main stair at Pittsburgh, a Piranesian composition of heavy Romanesque masonry arches framing a diagonal transitional space (fig. 4.5). For the same architectural feature at nearly the same time, Furness provided the Bryn Mawr Hotel (1890) in Pennsylvania with a delicate, freestanding stairway supported by exposed metallic I beams decoratively studded with rivet heads (fig. 4.6). An even more dramatic metallic stair was destroyed with the removal of the Baltimore and Ohio terminal in Philadelphia (1886–1888). On the one hand, we have an architecture of memory; on the other, of the machine. On the one hand, we have an evocation of the proven past; on the other, an emblem of the industrial present.

In the 1880s, Richardson and Furness designed identical building types in the libraries commissioned by, respectively, the University of Vermont and the University of Pennsylvania. The plans of the Billings Library (1883–1886) in Burlington and the Furness Library (1888–1890) in Philadelphia both evolved from ecclesiastical prototypes (although each is well adapted to its specific use). Richardson, as he did in all his library designs despite the pointed criticism of the American Library Association, created a building without the separate

4.5.

H. H. Richardson, Allegheny
County Courthouse, Pittsburgh,
1883–1888. Main stair. Photo by
Cervin Robinson.

4.6.

FURNESS, EVANS AND CO., Bryn
Mawr Hotel, 1890. Main stair. Photo
by Cervin Robinson.

and self-supporting metallic stacks that had been standard
since the middle of the 1870s. His preliminary study of the
wood-paneled and alcove-cluttered book room contemplates
an overhead structure of arched wooden braces and trusses (fig.
4.7). When the library was built, that proposal was changed to
a flat ceiling supported by exposed wooden girders and beams,
while the polygonal space for the Marsh Collection did retain
more of the original intent. That intent was to recall something of Merry Olde England.

4.7.

H. H. RICHARDSON, Billings Library,
University of Vermont, Burlington,
1883–1886. Preliminary study for the
reading room. From Mariana
Griswold Van Rensselaer, *Henry
Hobson Richardson and His Works*
(Boston: Houghton Mifflin, 1888).

4.8.

FURNESS, EVANS AND CO., Furness
Library, University of Pennsylvania,
Philadelphia, 1888–1890. Reading
room rotunda. Author's collection.

88

·

JAMES F.
O'GORMAN

In his library at the University of Pennsylvania, in contrast, Furness designed a separate wing for the books that incorporated freestanding metal and glass stacks beneath glass shed roofs. (The effect of this arrangement was eventually to cook the books printed on wood-pulp paper, but no one realized that until the next century.) He also supported the floor above the apsidal end, or rotunda, of the first-story reading room with emphatic steel beams radiating from the center of the space and curving down to meet, or to almost meet—a terra-cotta leaf intervenes—a series of brick piers encircling the room (fig. 4.8). The leaf-covered visual disjuncture between beam and support is a characteristic idiosyncratic touch, and one that imparts a sense of instability, of fictive kineticism, to Furness's design. Richardson invariably sought the reassuringly stable. While Furness's architectural use of

4.9.

H. H. RICHARDSON, Robert Treat
Paine house, Waltham, Mass., 1883–
1886. Exterior. Photo by Cervin
Robinson.

bare industrial structure was inspired by the recent writings of Eugène-Emmanuel Viollet-le-Duc and created a cutting-edge image, Richardson's design for the book room at Burlington harkens back to a distant past.

That such diverse agendas can be found throughout the work of these two men, whatever the building type under consideration, is demonstrated by next examining Richardson's Union passenger station (1885–1887) at New London, Connecticut, and Furness's Baltimore and Ohio terminal in Philadelphia. The former is a perfect example of Richardson's disciplined and quiet work. It is a balanced composition, all mass, all masonry: solid, conservative, reticent, well-bred. Although the railroad station is a quintessential nineteenth-century building type, nowhere in this building does the nineteenth century otherwise have much of an architectural impact. The massing and silhouette of the B & O terminal in contrast were all Sturm und Drang, all bluster and fury, all fuss and feathers. And all generated by nineteenth-century materials and technology. The lower wall of the Union Station is battered brick; the lower wall of the B & O was "principally of iron, carried on iron columns and boxes [i.e., box girders]."[6] The exposed metallic frame embraced flat planes, crisp corners, and hard edges building to an asymmetrical, picturesque composition. A completely industrial aesthetic also informed the interior of the station. If we must find in this era a progenitor of modernism, we should look to the B & O terminal, not the Union station. But what's the point?

One more comparison should suffice. Let's consider coeval domestic designs: domestic gable ends, for example, such as those of Richardson's Robert Treat Paine house and Furness's Samuel Shipley house (1882) in West Chester, Pennsylvania.

4.10.

FURNESS AND EVANS, Samuel

Shipley house, West Chester, Pa.,

1882. Exterior from the northwest.

Photo by Cervin Robinson.

Richardson's composition is vitalized by an interplay of symmetry and asymmetry but has an overall broad serenity and stability (fig. 4.9). Gravity clearly prevails as weight spreads outward from the low-pitched roof to the shingled upper walls to sturdy lower walls of hefty boulders to the ground. At the center of the composition is a Palladian window that opens into nothing more than a dressing room. A Palladian window: the touch of history! Paine's wife was a Lyman whose family owned Samuel McIntire's federal-style Vale at the bottom of the hill; Paine himself descended from a signer of the Declaration of Independence. The Palladian window, that most legible of classical emblems, tied the present generation to its illustrious forebears. Gravity and memory are the keynotes of the house.

At West Chester the composition seems to defy gravity (fig. 4.10). The clapboarded upper floor cantilevers right and left beyond the stone ground story while the brick chimney stack—which seems to rip through the tip of the gable—never visually reaches the ground. Rather, the brickwork rests at the top of the first story on a thin piece of slate supported by cantilevered iron I bars that are, in fact, railroad rails. Time-honored visual distribution of weight is abandoned here in favor of a demonstration of the gravity-defying possibilities of industrial material. The past (traditional brickwork) is visually upheld by an icon of the present (the nineteenth-century rail). Richardson's celebration of *then* is replaced by the liberating possibilities of *now*.

The nineteenth century comfortably embraced many dichotomies, and this might just be another: past and present, genesis and geology, art and industry, art and nature, nature and industry. Then and now, past and present, are not necessar-

·

JAMES F.
O'GORMAN

4.11.

CHILDE HASSAM, *Columbus Avenue,
Boston: Rainy Day,* 1885. Worcester Art
Museum, Worcester, Mass. Bequest
of Mrs. Charlotte E. W. Buffington.

ily exclusive, of course, as in the larger sense the present can be formed only out of the past; but this succinct polarity characterizes what the Banisterian method has revealed: very different intentions on the part of these two architects. If I have with this brief survey convinced you that there are significantly different—even diametrically opposed—agendas involved in the works of Richardson and Furness, you will want to ask what generated these distinctions. This is a question whose answer should take longer than I have here—in fact, I can barely hint at the richness of the subject—but I will point to one possible and I think determining root of the divergences we have noted.

Following our chosen methodology, we will look at another comparison, in this case a pair of urban vistas—one a view of Boston, the other a view of Philadelphia—for I want to suggest that the divergent agendas of Richardson and Furness were rooted in their divergent clienteles, which was a function of geography. The client orders architecture; the architect—even to some degree the signature architect—responds to the client's needs and wishes. The bases of architectural style are to be found as much in the profile of the client as in the education of the architect. Richardson worked—largely—for the Boston Brahmins, Furness for the Philadelphia industrialists and their circle. (This is a working generalization. We lack a detailed study of the client base of most nineteenth-century architects, a study that is much to be desired.)

Childe Hassam's genteel *Columbus Avenue, Boston: Rainy Day* (1885) shows the city's South End as a vista of boulevards, gracious architecture, pedestrians, carriages, and horsecars (fig. 4.11). The whole scene is slow-paced and bathed in a mistiness that suggests a timeless ambience. The industrial present is kept at arm's length: the tower rising in the right background

4.12.

JOSEPH PENNELL, *The Train Shed,*
Broad Street Station, ca. 1912. From
Joseph Pennell, *Joseph Pennell's*
Pictures of Philadelphia (Philadelphia:
Lippincott, 1926.)

marks Peabody and Stearns's 1872 Park Square railroad terminal.[7] Park Square had an impressive train shed, but Hassam's view obliterates it, and its tower in the artist's unfocused eye could as well be that of a civic or ecclesiastical building. This was a city of traditional materials, of human scale and human pace. This was the city of good breeding, of Henry James and William Dean Howells. This was the setting for a leadership significantly composed of men who, in the words of Edward S. Cooke, Jr., "were not manufacturing, railroad, or financial entrepreneurs but rather cultural capitalists, linked by common backgrounds, Harvard education, intermarriage, and good memberships."[8] It was a class of men who—like Richardson's clients, Robert Treat Paine, Francis Lee Higginson, or Henry Adams—rested heavily on the economic success of its ancestors, and who ruled "the museum, the academy, the dinner table, and the club" while railing against the new industrialists.[9]

Joseph Pennell's later image of Philadelphia stands in sharp contrast to the mood evoked by Hassam's Boston. In *The Train Shed, Broad Street Station,* a work from his turn-of-the-century series on the city, we stare awestruck into the huge shed of Furness's railroad terminal (fig. 4.12). And rightly so, for the 300-foot metallic trusses designed by Wilson Brothers and Company, "engineers and architects," made the structure the "largest single-span train-shed in the world" when it was completed in 1893.[10] It dwarfs the isolated figures in the foreground. Pennell's lithograph, like Claude Monet's earlier oils of stations in Paris, embraces nineteenth-century industry with gusto. Hassam's view of Boston pushed the railroad into the background; in Pennell's view, the icon of Philadelphia's history in the upper right corner, Alexander Milne Calder's colossal statue of William Penn atop the tower of the city and county buildings at Broad and Market Streets, is bullied into the background by the majestic creation of the cutting-edge engineer. Within the shed, the age of speed and the machine are evoked by the chugging and puffing Baldwin engines manufactured just a few blocks away.

Hassam and Pennell produced other views of Boston and Philadelphia that convey the same contrast. Although they are randomly chosen, *Columbus Avenue* and *Broad Street Station* accurately capture the essential differences between these cities in the nineteenth century. Boston was home to the genteel tradition. We've lost sight of the fact, but Philadelphia at that time, even more than Carl Sandburg's Chicago, was a "city of big shoulders," rawboned and bursting with industrial energy. The Baldwin Locomotive Company occupied a huge chunk of Center City. Furness's clients, men like Fairman Rogers, William Henszey, or Clement Griscom, were often engineers, industrialists, or the bankers and lawyers whose work centered on, say, the Pennsylvania Railroad. His engineering architecture felt right to them, for they too embraced the possibilities of their industrialized age.

H. H. Richardson developed a conservative architecture serving conservative Brahmin New England patronage. His beloved Romanesque style aptly fit his agenda as it was, like the Gothic, preindustrial; but unlike the Gothic, the Romanesque was materialistic, heavy-walled, undemonstrative, massively and traditionally load-bearing. It suggested solid, time-honored values; it created a reassuring sense of the past as present. Richardson joined John Ruskin and William Morris in harking back to the days of cottage industry and handicraft. He presented himself in the costume of a medieval monk; he surrounded himself with handwrought objects, including Rookwood pottery and De Morgan ceramics; and his surviving associates later organized and directed the retrospective Society of Arts and Crafts in Boston. Above all he eschewed the architectural expression of contemporary industrial production. He sought "quiet" in his buildings, the hush of clubby, ongoing, and well-bred social discourse.

Frank Furness laid aside Ruskin and Morris for Viollet-le-Duc. For the movers and shakers of highly mechanized Philadelphia, he created an engineer's aesthetic, an architecture that boldly expressed, through symbol and fact, the energy of Philadelphia's contemporary industrial production and technological innovation. His was an active architecture, the architectural equivalent of the city's hissing Baldwins. His works recognized the industrial revolution—as Richardson's did not. They celebrated the present. Where Richardson's buildings were quiet and massive, decorous and well-bred, Furness's were fragmented and noisy, aggressive and ill-mannered. They visually mimicked the shrill cry of the factory whistle as it echoed across the Quaker City.[11]

Richardson's work embodied the past: it was an architecture that celebrated memory. Furness's work embodied the present: it was an architecture that honored the machine. The era embraced both agendas. It was materialistic and conservative as well as industrial and daring. Past and present both inspired architecture of lasting importance. And in this recognition of both sides of the era's architecture, finally, we can identify Richardson's legacy. Despite a century of rhetoric to the contrary, it is now clear that in the hands of a gifted designer, conservative as well as cutting-edge architecture can rise to the highest level of achievement. Deep-seated materialism is the key to understanding the quality of Richardson's accomplishment. That Richardson's work never went into eclipse during the middle of the twentieth century—as did Furness's—was due not to its prescience but to its presence.

Notes

1. Some recent references are James F. O'Gorman, *Living Architecture: A Biography of H. H. Richardson* (New York: Simon and Schuster, 1997); James F. O'Gorman, *H. H. Richardson: Architectural Forms for an American Society* (Chicago: University of Chicago Press, 1987); Jeffrey Karl Ochsner, *H. H. Richardson: Complete Architectural Works* (Cambridge, Mass.: MIT Press, 1982); George E. Thomas, Michael J. Lewis, and Jeffrey A. Cohen, *Frank Furness: The Complete Works* (New York: Princeton Architectural Press, 1991); and James F. O'Gorman, *The Architecture of Frank Furness* (Philadelphia: Philadelphia Museum of Art, 1973).

2. For a brief note on some other differences, see James F. O'Gorman, "Furness and Richardson: A Tale of Two Interiors," *Nineteenth Century* 14 (1994): 32–36.

3. James F. O'Gorman, *Three American Architects: Richardson, Sullivan, and Wright, 1865–1915* (Chicago: University of Chicago Press, 1991). The last sentence of this book, for example, rather than pointing to the future, curls the whole study back on itself. It returns the entire episode to its early-nineteenth-century origins.

4. This was of course not Furness's invention. His Philadelphia precursor, William Strickland, made extensive architectural use of exposed iron details as early as the 1830s (as in the New Orleans mint). The metal could then be exposed—as it now cannot—because it was considered to be of itself "fireproof."

5. An observation I owe to the late Margaret Henderson Floyd.

6. Thomas, Lewis, and Cohen, *Frank Furness,* 268, quoting *The Builder's Guide.*

7. Carroll Louis Vanderslice Meeks, *The Railroad Station: An Architectural History* (New Haven: Yale University Press, 1956), 87, 101.

8. Edward S. Cooke, Jr., "Talking or Working; The Conundrum of Moral Aesthetics in Boston's Arts and Crafts Movement," in *Inspiring Reform: Boston's Arts and Crafts Movement,* by Marilee Boyd Meyer et al. (Wellesley, Mass.: Davis Museum and Cultural Center, Wellesley College; New York: dist. by Harry N. Abrams, 1997), 19. Cooke cites one standard work: Ronald Story, *The Forging of an Aristocracy: Harvard and the Boston Upper Class,* 1800–1870 (Middletown, Conn.: Wesleyan University Press, 1980).

9. Mona Domosh, *Invented Cities: The Creation of Landscape in Nineteenth-Century New York and Boston* (New Haven: Yale University Press, 1996), 125. Domosh cites another standard work: Frederic Cople Jaher, *The Urban Establishment: Upper Strata in Boston, New York, Charleston, Chicago, and Los Angeles* (Urbana, Ill.: University of Illinois Press, 1982).

10. Meeks, *Railroad Station,* 103; Elizabeth Robins Pennell and Joseph Pennell, *Our Philadelphia* (Philadelphia: J. P. Lippincott, 1914), 99.

11. George E. Thomas of Philadelphia has taught me much about Furness's architecture as a reflection of Furness's city.

5

SEEING RICHARDSON
IN HIS TIME:
The Problem of the
Romanesque Revival

Jeffrey Karl Ochsner

I n looking backward, architectural historians create narratives that emphasize particular events because they lead to known conclusions. But because this process is selective, the historian of architecture must recognize the inherent tension between the desire to create a structured narrative framework and the desire to recognize and present the more complex and even diffuse context in which design decisions were actually made during a given period. This conflict presents a challenge to those who wish to see the work of Henry Hobson Richardson as it was seen in his own time—the 1880s and early 1890s. Moreover, that same difficulty is the major impediment to our understanding and appreciating the architecture Richardson influenced—variously identified as "Richardsonian Romanesque," "Romanesque revival," or simply "Richardsonian."

Our understanding of Richardson today differs radically from that of his contemporaries for two primary reasons. First, we have seen the architecture that came after Richardson—that is, we already know how the next chapters of architectural history unfold. Second, we see Richardson and his work through the eyes of the critics, historians, and others who have already written about his work. They have told us which works are the important ones and which are less important, which are the harbingers of subsequent developments in architecture and which would lead only to dead ends. Their evaluations of Richardson both inform our vision and stand in the way of our gaining insights into Richardson's influence in his time.

The problem is exemplified by the treatment in architectural history of Richardson's Oakes Ames Memorial Hall, North Easton, Massachusetts (1879–1881; fig. 5.1). In 1936 Henry-Russell Hitchcock, in *The Architecture of H. H. Richardson and His Times,* called it "unworthy of [Richardson's] genius," describing it as "an awkward and aggressive pile" that was "not successful" as architecture. Hitchcock criticized every aspect—the proportions of the tower, the contrast and use of materials, the building's monumentality, and the composition of the roof and dormers. He did praise the building's picturesque siting and general massing, but otherwise he characterized the structure as "a lapse and an anachronism" that was "not up to the standard."[1]

Yet during the 1880s and 1890s, Memorial Hall was one of Richardson's best known and most highly regarded buildings. In 1885, it was included on the list of the ten best buildings in America compiled by *American Architect and Building News*

5.1.

H. H. RICHARDSON, Oakes Ames
Memorial Hall, North Easton,
Mass., 1879–1881. Photo from
American Architect and Building News 13
(19 May 1883). Courtesy of the
Trustees of the Boston
Public Library.

from a survey of architects (discussed below). Even Hitchcock admitted, "This was one of Richardson's most generally admired buildings," but he then commented that "the American public has always had an unerring flair for what is just behind the times" and dismissed the architects whose work showed its influence as "second rate."[2]

Reading Hitchcock, we might assume that Richardson, too, saw Memorial Hall as a misstep—as a lesser work. Yet available evidence suggests otherwise. More than four years after the completion of Memorial Hall, Richardson chose a photograph of it as the first image of his work sent to his new Chicago clients, the Glessners, when he wrote to them in May 1885.[3] Would Richardson have sent a photograph of a building he regarded as inferior? Or one representing a direction that he was abandoning? We would do well to reconsider what we have been led to believe about the direction of Richardson's work.

QUESTIONING THE STANDARD NARRATIVE

As noted by James F. O'Gorman in the introduction to his *Selected Drawings: H. H. Richardson and His Office* (1974), and as expanded by Margaret Henderson Floyd in her *Architecture after Richardson: Regionalism before Modernism—Longfellow, Alden, and Harlow in Boston and Pittsburgh* (1994), the narrative framework of late-nineteenth-century American architectural history that most historians still teach and most students still learn was largely constructed by Lewis Mumford and Henry-Russell Hitchcock in the 1920s and 1930s.[4] Both Mumford and Hitchcock were seeking American roots for a modern architecture like that which they had seen in Europe. Although Mumford presented Richardson as "the first architect of distinction in America who was ready to face the totality of modern life," it was Hitchcock's 1936 study that offered the explanatory framework that continues to shape how Richardson and his times are understood.[5]

As O'Gorman wrote in 1974, Hitchcock's underlying aim was "to establish Richardson as the father of the International Style."[6] And Hitchcock's emphases clearly display his modernist biases, whether in his appreciation of the plain, unadorned wall surfaces of the Brattle Square Church, the back wall of the Bryant house, or the Allegheny County Jail (rather than the Allegheny Courthouse itself); his dismissal of the Glessner house's Arts and Crafts interiors (now known to be of Richardson's design); his praise of the horizontal bands of windows at the Crane Library; or his comparison of the Bryant house bridge to the work of Le Corbusier.[7] Following Hitchcock, critics have generally interpreted Richardson as a proto-modern designer whose work moved from eclecticism to the brink of modern architecture. Within this interpretation, Hitchcock argued that Richardson's influence on Louis Sullivan was his only significant legacy. Other understandings of Richardson's achievement were seen as "almost meaningless."[8]

Nonetheless, this dominant narrative has not gone unchallenged. Floyd has noted that O'Gorman's 1974 study of Richardson's drawings should be credited with opening the door to a reevaluation.[9] In his introduction, O'Gorman focused on the production of Richardson's designs through the teamwork characteristic of an architect's office: "It takes nothing away from Richardson's stature as an architect to envision him as part of a group of interacting individuals who together contributed to the work we for convenience call *his*."[10] In *Architecture after Richardson,* Floyd observed that Hitchcock was able to present Richardson as a lone proto-modern genius because he routinely blamed the nonmodern features of Richardson's buildings (the features he did not like) on the office staff.[11] While Hitchcock characterized early staff members such as Stanford White as "one-eyed," the later staff members were entirely "blind." He routinely referred to the "inferiority of the office staff" and argued that Richardson's contemporaries and followers showed an "almost total incapacity" to understand his work.[12] But Hitchcock made significant mistakes in developing this narrative: an example is his crediting the "very poor" Glessner interiors to the staff, whereas we now know that Richardson was fully responsible for them; furthermore, the Glessners' library was modeled directly on the library in Richardson's own office. Hitchcock also celebrated the granite exterior, and we now know that Richardson wanted marble—the granite was selected by the Glessners after Richardson's death.[13] These are just a few examples, but they show that Hitchcock's evaluations were *his* own and they suggest that he may have misunderstood Richardson's intentions.

In this context, Floyd has argued that the familiar linear narrative of late-nineteenth-century American architectural history should be replaced by a fan-shaped radial topology in which Richardson should be seen as a font of inspiration generating work in a variety of directions.[14] Floyd's model promises a better accounting of Richardson's influence and recognizes the variety of architectural achievements in the period between the Civil War and the turn of the century.

Therefore, a reconsideration of the years after 1865 will still find Richardson in a central role, but Hitchcock's 1930s interpretation of Richardson must be completely set aside. With their after-the-fact dismissal of most late-nineteenth-century American architecture, Hitchcock, Mumford and others stand in the way of seeing the work of the period as it was seen then. Their explanations of Richardson's designs were not cast in terms that Richardson used to explain his own work, nor in terms that were used by Richardson's contemporaries. If the "Richardsonian" architectural production across the United States is to be understood, it must be placed in the context of its own time. Indeed, a logically valid analysis of American architecture between 1865 and 1895 can only be made in terms of the *choices actually made by architects at the time*, not by applying the principles of 1930s modernism (principles that neither Richardson nor any of his contemporaries could have predicted) to 1880s architecture.

RICHARDSON AS SEEN IN HIS TIME

Once we have set aside twentieth-century interpretations of Richardson as a proto-modernist, we must turn to nineteenth-century presentations of his achievements to understand how architects responded to his work in its time. The positive contemporary perception of Richardson's work is evident first in the selection of five of his buildings for the 1885 *American Architect* list of the ten best buildings in the United States: Trinity Church (1872–1877) in Boston; Sever Hall (1878–1880) at Harvard University; Memorial Hall (1879–1881) in North Easton; Albany City Hall (1880–1882); and the New York State Capitol (1872–1886) in Albany.[15] These five buildings represent some of the different directions in Richardson's work. The selection was made before the completion of Allegheny County buildings (1883–1888) in Pittsburgh, the Marshall Field Wholesale Store (1885–1887) in Chicago, and the Cincinnati Chamber of Commerce building (1885–1888). Had these well-publicized late works been finished, this list might have

5.2.

H. H. Richardson, Trinity Church,

Boston, 1872–1877. Photo from

American Architect and Building News 2

(3 February 1877). Courtesy of the

Trustees of the Boston Public

Library.

changed, but even then it probably would not have centered on a single direction in Richardson's work. Indeed, this list suggests that contemporary architects could take very different signals from Richardson's buildings: Trinity Church could be seen as an example of historical eclecticism (fig. 5.2); Memorial Hall as a model of picturesque Queen Anne/Arts and Crafts design; Sever Hall as a building distinguished by simplification, symmetrical balance, and restrained detail; and Albany City Hall as a design that was similar to Memorial Hall but simplified, with a tower that could be interpreted as a residual picturesque element.[16]

Richardson's late works displayed similar variation. The Marshall Field Wholesale Store has always been celebrated for its proto-modernity and its influence on Chicago architects, but the Allegheny County Courthouse received far more publicity when it was completed.[17] Though Hitchcock and other modernist historians preferred the Allegheny County Jail, in the late 1880s the Courthouse attracted the most attention and the most imitators (fig. 5.3). The Cincinnati Chamber of Commerce building, although denigrated by Hitchcock, attracted attention because of the initial competition; illustrations of the Cincinnati building appeared in *American Architect* and in other publications, including *Inland Architect* in 1889 and *Architectural Record* in 1891 (fig. 5.4).[18]

The vertical emphasis of both the Allegheny County Courthouse and the Cincinnati Chamber of Commerce building would have looked familiar to nineteenth-century observers. The kind of "ground-hugging" horizontal emphasis of buildings such as Richardson's railroad stations was not particularly evident in his larger public buildings. Buildings such as Richardson's railroad stations and his shingled houses were

5.3.

H. H. RICHARDSON, Allegheny
County Courthouse and Jail,
Pittsburgh, 1883–1888. Photo from
Inland Architect 13 (May 1889).
Courtesy of the Trustees of the
Boston Public Library.

5.4.

H. H. RICHARDSON, Cincinnati

Chamber of Commerce, 1885–1888

(destroyed). Drawing from

Architectural Record 1

(October–December 1891).

almost never illustrated in photographs in the architectural press.[19] And, although some of these did appear in Mariana Griswold Van Rensselaer's 1888 biography, *Henry Hobson Richardson and His Works*, her book was initially issued in only 500 copies. The influence of the book was limited to a small circle, and even its illustrations present a variety of directions in Richardson's work, not a single evolutionary thread.[20]

The multiple directions in Richardson's work were further emphasized by its publication in *American Architect and Building News*. Illustrations did not come to an end when Richardson died: in fact, images appeared more frequently in the first years after his death than previously.[21] These images were not published in chronological order, and their very randomness made clear the diversity of Richardson's work. For example, the Winn Library (1876–1879) in Woburn, Massachusetts, appeared in May 1886, after the Ames Library (1877–1879) in North Easton and the Crane Library (1880–1882) in Quincy, both of which appeared in 1883.[22] Because each building's date was not included, the sequence of development would not have been evident to most contemporary readers.[23] Indeed, the buildings published between early 1885 and late 1886, including the Ames Gate Lodge (1880–1881) in North Easton, Austin Hall (1881–1884) at Harvard, the Winn Library, and the Ames Store (1882–1883) on Bedford Street in Boston, were far from presenting Richardson as a proto-modernist.[24] The buildings subsequently published by *American Architect* included the Albany City Hall (twice), the Cincinnati Chamber of Commerce building (twice), and the Allegheny County Courthouse (five times between 1890 and 1895), but the journal never published the Field store.[25] Similarly, *American Architect* published the Sard house, Albany

(1882–1885), in 1889; the Warder house, Washington (1885–1888), in 1891; and the MacVeagh house, Chicago (1885–1887), in 1893—but never the Glessner house (1885–1887), which of these is probably the most highly regarded today.[26] Of Richardson's nonmasonry buildings, the only one to appear was the Sherman house in October 1887, after it had been expanded by Stanford White. In this case Richardson was presented as a Queen Anne architect, not an advanced shingle-style designer.[27] The popularity of the images of Richardson's buildings led the *American Architect*'s publisher to offer groups of images in folios. Austin Hall at Harvard was the first to be featured in 1886; Richardson's buildings in North Easton, with an emphasis on Memorial Hall, were the subject of the third folio, also published in 1886; Trinity Church was the focus of the fifth folio, published in 1888; a separate folio of images of the Billings Library, not in the same series, was issued as well.[28]

Inland Architect, the Chicago-based publication widely distributed in the Midwest and West, also carried images of Richardson's buildings, but only those outside New England. The Marshall Field Store was presented in a single view in October 1888, the Cincinnati Chamber of Commerce building received four images in January 1889, and ten views of Allegheny County Courthouse appeared in May and June 1889. Between 1887 and 1889, *Inland Architect* also carried illustrations of six Richardson houses, including two in Washington (the Adams house of 1884–1886 and the Warder house), two in Chicago (the MacVeagh and Glessner houses), the J. R. Lionberger house (1885–1888) in St. Louis, and the Gratwick house (1886–1889) in Buffalo.[29]

Richardson was not seen then in isolation from the other architects of his time, yet most historians have so tended to regard him.[30] Historians have studied Richardson's buildings in chronological order to examine the evolution of his career, in general focusing on him to the exclusion of others. Thus, we now know far more about Richardson than architects of his day knew. By isolating Richardson's work, we have made our study of his career easier and enabled ourselves to present a coherent narrative of his designs. Such isolation, however, is artificial. Architects in Richardson's time saw Richardson as a great architect, but they saw his work as part of a continuum of contemporary projects. Between 1878 and 1892, Richardson was well published, with about forty-two images of his buildings appearing in *American Architect and Building News*. Yet during that period *American Architect* published well over 3,500 illustrations, by my estimate, so Richardson's work was less than 1.2 percent of the total.[31]

How then should we regard Richardson? Some historians have identified a "proto-modern Richardson." But clearly there are other Richardsons. There is a "picturesque Richardson"; there is also a "shingle-style Richardson"—the work characterized at the time as "modern colonial"; the Glessner house interiors reflect an "Arts and Crafts Richardson." We can also identify Richardson as an American Victorian architect and as a Romanesque eclectic architect—after all, *American Architect* published an image of the Trinity Church tower in December 1887, fully ten years after it was completed; the editors must have thought their readers would find it of interest.[32]

To see Richardson in this way is to see a different Richardson: a more complex architect, but one who is more real. It makes him less the prescient genius that Hitchcock claimed and more an architect of his time. This analysis speaks more directly to how change in architecture really occurs and how architects struggle to make good buildings. Echoing O'Gorman's 1974 statement about Richardson as the leader of a design team, we can say: It takes nothing away from his stature to see Richardson as an architect who worked within but nonetheless mastered the tendencies of his time, who produced work that was sometimes complex and sometimes even contradictory, and who occasionally pushed the envelope of architectural design in a variety of directions that inspired the architects of his generation. This vision of Richardson allows us to understand why he inspired so many responses—and shows why Floyd's fan-shaped topology is an appropriate model of his influence.

THE INFLUENCE OF H. H. RICHARDSON

Richardson rarely wrote about his work, and he never addressed his design ideas in the general circulation architectural press.[33] In this silence he contrasts markedly with other American architectural leaders, who frequently were prolific writers—John W. Root, Louis Sullivan, and Frank Lloyd Wright. They provided frameworks through which to see their buildings. Because Richardson offered so little commentary on his own work, architects in his time were able to project interpretations on it.[34] What Richardson's contemporaries found in his work, whether reading the architectural journals or, in a few cases, actually visiting the buildings, depended very strongly on what they brought to it. Those whose training was in the American High Victorian modes perceived in Richardson what they already knew. Those who had academic backgrounds viewed Richardson from that standpoint. The

5.5.

ELMER H. FISHER, Pioneer Building,
Seattle, 1889–1892. Photo. Courtesy of
the Manuscripts, Archives, and
Special Collections Division,
University of Washington Libraries.

diverse directions of Richardson's works as seen through publications provided the opportunity for each architect to understand Richardson differently. The result, therefore, is the wide variety of directions in the work in the 1880s and 1890s—work sometimes characterized as "Richardsonian." The number of Richardsonian buildings produced in that period is broad but a few will suffice to make the point.

The Pioneer Building, Seattle (1889–1892), by local architect Elmer H. Fisher, was one of the business blocks erected in the city after a fire in June 1889 destroyed the downtown (fig. 5.5). In October 1889, as new buildings were beginning to rise, Fisher stated explicitly in a local paper that the new buildings were "Romanesque, after the example of the great architect of America, Mr. Richardson."[35] The Pioneer Building was one of Fisher's finest creations, but we would hardly characterize it as Richardsonian. Fisher's background was in building and contracting; having spent most of his time in the West, he had limited experience in big cities. His architectural career began only in the mid-1880s in British Columbia. When he arrived in Seattle in 1888, he designed in the American High Victorian modes, and many of his business buildings show the contemporary tendency to grid façades with pilasters and belt courses and to treat a large block as a series of adjacent vertical pavilions. When Fisher started to design buildings after the example of Richardson, he could not escape his background. Thus, his work is best described as American High Victorian with Richardsonian motifs. It is impossible to know whether Fisher had ever seen one of Richardson's buildings, but he appears to have followed at least some architectural journals, as he later published work in the Minneapolis-based *Northwestern Architect*.[36]

·

JEFFREY KARL

OCHSNER

5.6.

JOHN LYMAN FAXON, Newton

Centre Baptist Church, Newton,

Mass., 1887–1889. From "American

Buildings: Selections," vol. 3, pl. 26

(originally published in *Inland*

Architect 13 [April 1889]). Courtesy

Avery Architectural and Fine Arts

Library, Columbia University in the

City of New York.

_____

ACCEPTED·DESIGN·FOR
CAMBRIDGE·CITY·HALL

Longfellow Alden & Harlow.
Architects

5.7.

LONGFELLOW, ALDEN AND HARLOW,

Cambridge City Hall, Cambridge,

Mass., 1888–1889. Drawing from

American Architect and Building News 24

(28 July 1888). Courtesy of the

Trustees of the Boston Public

Library.

Architects who knew Richardson's work firsthand also produced varied interpretations. One example is the Newton Centre, Massachusetts, Baptist Church (1887–1889) by John Lyman Faxon, a work Hitchcock initially identified as Richardson's (although he corrected this error in subsequent editions of his book).[37] Hitchcock was critical of this work for the awkward juxtapositions of the parts and the free combination of elements and details from different Richardson buildings (fig. 5.6). Faxon clearly saw Richardson as a picturesque eclectic architect, and he copied the assembly of a series of related masses evident in Richardson's designs for the Winn Library and Trinity Church. Again, rather than condemning the Newton Centre church as inferior, we might ask what background Faxon brought to his design and through what framework he saw Richardson.[38] We should also recognize that this building was well enough regarded at the time to appear in *Inland Architect* in a photograph.[39]

Finally, the Cambridge, Massachusetts, City Hall (1888–1889), by Longfellow, Alden and Harlow, shows a more strongly disciplined, academic approach. A drawing of the competition-winning design appeared in *American Architect* in July 1888 (fig. 5.7).[40] A. W. Longfellow, Jr., who had been educated at the Ecole des Beaux-Arts, emerged as one of Richardson's chief assistants in the early 1880s. Thus the stronger academic direction with clear symmetries and studied proportions evident in this Richardsonian design are not surprising. Ultimately, of course, for Longfellow the academic eclectic approach inherent in Richardson's work was to prove much more important than its "Richardsonian language."[41]

These are only three examples, but they serve to illustrate the point: the architects of the time projected on Richardson's diverse output their own interpretations and produced a variety of works that they thought were following Richardson's example—and they were, each in his own way.

BUILDING TYPES

The variety of building types it encompassed also made Richardson's work a good source for architects in the 1880s and 1890s. Those were years of rapid city building in the West and urban expansion in the East, growth accompanied by an increasing variety of building types requiring architectural design. Architectural historians have often remarked that Richardson was one of the earliest architects to respond to the new building types—such as the small-town library and the large urban business block.[42] To architects of that time, Richardsonian architecture appeared to offer a clear system that could be applied to most of the design problems they faced. His architectural language both was widely applicable and offered a range of solutions to the building tasks faced by architects in an urbanizing America.

For business blocks in the burgeoning cities, Richardson's primary examples were the Ames stores on Bedford Street and on Harrison Avenue (1886–1887), both in Boston and both published in *American Architect*, and the Marshall Field Store, published in *Inland Architect*.[43] Many cities at the time were adopting new fire ordinances that required masonry construction in their downtowns; architects turned to the "Richardsonian system" to give their buildings an appropriate architectural character. The Richardsonian Romanesque showed the way to achieve a powerful architectural image of strength and stability without the elaborate decorative treatment typical in the United States in the 1870s and 1880s

JEFFREY KARL

OCHSNER

5.8.

SHEPLEY, RUTAN AND COOLIDGE,
Lionberger Wholesale Warehouse, St.
Louis, 1887–1889 (destroyed). Drawing
from *American Architect and Building
News* 21 (21 May 1887). Courtesy of the
Trustees of the Boston Public Library.

5.9.

HARRY W. JONES, National Bank of
Commerce Building, Minneapolis,
1887–1888 (destroyed). Photo from
Northwestern Architect 7 (May 1889).
Courtesy of the Library of Congress,
Washington, D.C.

5.10.

JOHN PARKINSON, Seattle National
Bank Building, Seattle, 1890–1892.
Drawing from *American Architect and
Building News* 28 (5 July 1890).
Courtesy of the Manuscripts, Archives,
and Special Collections Division,
University of Washington Libraries.

(whether Gothic revival or Second Empire). Many published works derived from Richardson's business buildings. For example, Richardson's successor firm, Shepley, Rutan and Coolidge, was responsible for the Lionberger Wholesale Warehouse (1887–1889) in St. Louis, which shows the direct influence of the Field store. A drawing of it was published in *American Architect* (fig. 5.8), and a photograph appeared in *Architectural Record.* The firm's F. L. Ames Building (1889–1891), Boston, also published in *American Architect,* was another commercial block derived from Richardson's example.[44] The Field store was also a primary source for the National Bank of Commerce Building, Minneapolis (1887–1888), by Harry W. Jones. Jones had attended MIT and very likely worked for Richardson in 1883. His Bank of Commerce was published in *Northwestern Architect* in 1889 (fig. 5.9).[45]

Architects could use the Richardsonian system without having been trained in Richardson's office. George B. Post, among the leaders in the design of office buildings in New York, was responsible for several essays in the mode, notably the New York Times Building (1888–1889), which appeared in *Architectural Record,* and the Union Trust Company (1889–1890), which appeared in both *American Architect* and *Architectural Record.*[46] John Parkinson's Seattle National Bank Building (1890–1892), which appeared in *American Architect* in July 1890 (fig. 5.10), and William Boone's New York Block (1889–1892), also in Seattle, demonstrate the reach of Richardson's example to the West Coast.[47]

For large public buildings, Richardson's most influential work was the Allegheny County Courthouse, and the Albany City Hall was occasionally imitated as well. In states in the West, the 1880s and 1890s were years of significant investment in new public buildings—particularly county courthouses. Fireproof construction for storage of permanent public records was a major concern, and masonry buildings were the answer. Richardson's work provided the model for many of these buildings. Probably one of the finest of the Richardsonian courthouses was the Minneapolis Municipal Building and Hennepin County Courthouse (1888–1906), by Long and Kees, published in both *American Architect* and *Northwestern Architect* in 1888 (fig. 5.11).[48] Other notable examples include the Pierce County Courthouse, Tacoma (1890–1893), by Proctor and Dennis, published in *Northwestern Architect* in 1890; the Los Angeles County Courthouse (1886–1891), by Curtlett, Eisen and Cuthbertson, published in *Architectural Record* in 1891 (fig. 5.12); and the many courthouses in Texas designed by James Riely Gordon.[49] U.S. courthouses and other federal buildings designed by the Office of the Supervising Architect of the U.S. Treasury also frequently displayed the Richardson language after Mifflin E. Bell became supervising architect in 1884. The San Antonio Post Office and Courthouse (1887–1889), published in *American Architect,* is a typical example; the design is a picturesque composition in a Richardsonian vocabulary, and the source for the tower was Richardson's Brattle Square Church.[50]

In the East and Midwest, urban and suburban growth required new public buildings on a smaller scale—new libraries, new railroad stations, and other similar structures: Richardson's smaller public buildings provided good models. His suburban libraries had been well published in *American Architect*. As the public library movement flourished, many more small libraries of masonry with simplified Romanesque details appeared. Examples published in *American Architect* include libraries in Richmond, Vermont; Lexington,

5.11.

LONG AND KEES, Minneapolis
Municipal Building and Hennepin
County Courthouse, Minneapolis,
1888–1906. Drawing from
Northwestern Architect 6 (August 1888).
Courtesy of the Minneapolis Public
Library.

5.12.

CURTLETT, EISEN AND
CUTHBERTSON, Los Angeles County
Courthouse, 1886–1891 (destroyed).
Drawing from *Architectural Record* 1
(July-September 1891).

————————

Kentucky; Acton, Massachusetts; New London, Connecticut;
and Cambridge, Massachusetts (fig. 5.13).[51] Richardson's railroad stations had not been well published, but Shepley, Rutan
and Coolidge continued to receive station commissions from
the Boston and Albany Railroad and effected a seamless transition from Richardson's designs to their own work in this type,
both for the Boston and Albany and for other lines. Their large
station for the Boston and Albany (1888–1891) at Springfield,
Massachusetts, was published in *American Architect* and in

———————

Architectural Record.[52] The Richardsonian system could also be applied to other small public building types. One example is Arthur Vinal's Boston Water Works (1887–1888) in Chestnut Hill, Massachusetts. It was well enough regarded in its time that it was published in multiple views in *Northwestern Architect* in 1889 (fig. 5.14).[53]

Indeed, only Richardson's residential architecture was less influential. Architectural periodicals rarely published his houses.

His masonry houses offered useful models only for houses of the wealthy in the largest metropolitan centers such as Boston, New York, Pittsburgh, Detroit, Chicago, Minneapolis, and St. Louis.[54] In most places, residential construction remained wood frame, and the Queen Anne and "modern colonial" (now shingle-style) modes were common, but neither was considered "Richardsonian" in the same way as the masonry Romanesque revival.

SEEING RICHARDSON IN THE 1880S AND 1890S

To see Richardson within the context of his time, we must challenge familiar narratives that have isolated his life and work. His stature is not lessened if he is reevaluated in the context of his age. Indeed, to view Richardson in this way is to see a vital and prolific designer. He was an experimenter whose work moved in a variety of directions and who clearly reached beyond the design conventions of his contemporaries. Complex and varied, Richardson was an inspiration for a generation of designers.

If Richardson's buildings are seen as immersed in the architecture of the period, then the work of the architects who turned to Richardson's example can be more fairly evaluated in terms of their own accomplishments. To understand Richardson's contemporaries, we need to understand both the variety of Richardson's own work and the wide range of influences shaping architecture at the time. We should also recognize how difficult it is for architects in any period to see beyond the wide array of available imagery found in the professional journals to discover underlying trends or broad design tendencies.

The Richardsonian Romanesque provided an adaptable system of design through which architects in the period were able to address the multiple new building tasks that they faced. The Romanesque revival was a successful mode of design that addressed pragmatic requirements for fire-resistive construction and applicability to a wide array of building types; it also provided an aesthetic system representing stability, soundness, and strength. Yet this architecture remains relatively unstudied. At least in part, such neglect has resulted from viewing these buildings through a narrative framework that would not allow us to see their value. But if we reconsider these works in the context of their time, we can begin to appreciate the complex richness in the achievements of the architecture we characterize as "Richardsonian." We can begin to evaluate these works on their own terms, not just as designs that may fail to equal Richardson's own achievement. And we can begin to understand and celebrate the legacy left behind by the architects who were inspired by Richardson's example.

Notes

1. Henry-Russell Hitchcock, *The Architecture of H. H. Richardson and His Times* rev. ed. (1961; reprint, Cambridge, Mass.: MIT Press, 1966), 197–198, 199 (1st ed. published in 1936).

2. Ibid., 199.

3. On his return from Chicago after his first meeting with John J. and Frances Glessner, Richardson wrote to thank them for their hospitality, and with his letter he enclosed a photograph of Oakes Ames Memorial Hall. Receipt of this photograph is noted by Frances Glessner in her diary; she calls the building "Oakes Ames lodge," apparently in reference to its use as a lodge hall. See Frances M. Glessner, 25 May 1885, "Journals (1879–1921) of Frances Glessner," Archives and Manuscripts Department, Chicago Historical Society.

4. James F. O'Gorman, *H. H. Richardson and His Office: A Centennial of His Move to Boston, 1874: Selected Drawings* (Cambridge, Mass.: Department of Printing and Graphic Arts, Harvard College Library, 1974), 31; Margaret Henderson Floyd, *Architecture after Richardson: Regionalism before Modernism—Longfellow, Alden, and Harlow in Boston and Pittsburgh* (Chicago: University of Chicago Press and Pittsburgh History and Landmarks Foundation, 1994), 5–10.

5. Lewis Mumford, *Sticks and Stones: A Study of American Architecture and Civilization* (New York: Boni and Liveright, 1924) and *The Brown Decades*, 2nd ed. (New York: Dover, 1955), 118.

6. O'Gorman, *Selected Drawings*, 31.

7. Hitchcock, *Richardson and His Times*, 114 (Brattle Square Church), 207 (Bryant house), 210–211 (Crane Library), 259 (Allegheny County Jail), 278 (Glessner house).

8. Ibid., 290. James F. O'Gorman's *H. H. Richardson: Architectural Forms for an American Society* (Chicago: University of Chicago Press, 1987) places Richardson's work in a different context, interpreting its development in relationship to the American landscape. But O'Gorman, too, dismisses virtually all of Richardson's influence except that on architects in Chicago (see 67–68, 127–128). In a later book, *Three American Architects: Richardson, Sullivan, and Wright, 1865–1915* (Chicago: University of Chicago Press, 1991), O'Gorman returns to the dominant narrative, although arguing not that these architects should all be seen as precursors to modernism but rather that they were all rooted in the nineteenth century.

9. Floyd, *Architecture after Richardson*, 8–9.

10. O'Gorman, *Selected Drawings*, 29–30.

11. Floyd, *Architecture after Richardson*, 5–8.

12. Hitchcock, *Richardson and His Times*, 163–164, 128, 241.

13. For Hitchcock's critique of the Glessner interiors, see *Richardson and His Times*, 278. However, Richardson's involvement in the project, including the design of the interiors, is amply documented. In fact, when Richardson met for the last time with the Glessners (11 February 1886) he noted the position of the gaslights on the interior elevations. Thus, the design for the interiors was completed more

than two months before Richardson's death. The substitution of granite for marble on the exterior was made by the Glessners in July 1886. See Mary Alice Molloy, "Richardson's Web: A Client's Assessment of the Architect's Home and Studio," *Journal of the Society of Architectural Historians* 54 (March 1995): 18–19, 21.

14. Floyd, *Architecture after Richardson,* 10.

15. *American Architect and Building News* 17 (13 June 1885): 282.

16. The fifth project that could be identified with Richardson, the New York State Capitol, was the creation of multiple architects working over a period of more than thirty years. Because the design reflected its many participants, what contemporary architects took from the inclusion of this building on the list of the "ten best" is unclear. For general background on the New York State Capitol, see Jeffrey Karl Ochsner, *H. H. Richardson: Complete Architectural Works,* rev. ed. (Cambridge, Mass.: MIT Press, 1984), 157–167.

17. The Allegheny County buildings were the most frequently illustrated structures by Richardson, with ten images in *Inland Architect* in May and June 1889 and five images in *American Architect and Building News* between May 1890 and October 1895.

18. After Richardson's death, sketches of his most significant buildings appeared in *American Architect and Building News* 20 (11 September 1886). The competition entry for the Cincinnati Chamber of Commerce was among the buildings illustrated. A revised drawing of the Cincinnati Chamber of Commerce appeared in *Architectural Record* 1 (October–December 1891): 158. Subsequently photographs of details and the interior of the building were published; see below, notes 25 and 29.

19. Of Richardson's railroad stations, the only one photographed in the professional journals was the Boston and Albany Railroad Station at Chestnut Hill (1883–1884), which appeared in *American Architect and Building News* 16 (13 December 1884). After Richardson's death, a series of sketches of some of his stations appeared in *American Architect and Building News* 20 (11 September 1886). Additional sketches were included in *American Architect and Building News* 21 (2 February 1887); however, they conveyed limited information and should not be con-

sidered equivalent to the full-page or half-page plates published by the journal.

Although Richardson's shingled houses never appeared in a professional journal, the M. F. Stoughton house, Cambridge, Mass., of 1882–1883 was included in two contemporary books: George W. Sheldon, *Artistic Country Seats: Types of Recent American Villa and Cottage Architecture with Instances of Country Club-houses* (1886–1887; facsimile reprint, New York: Da Capo, 1979), 1:157; and Russell Sturgis et al., *Homes in City and Country* (New York: C. Scribner's Sons, 1893), 84–85.

20. Mariana Griswold Van Rensselaer, *Henry Hobson Richardson and His Works* (Boston: Houghton Mifflin, 1888). There are two facsimile reprints, one with an introduction by James D. Van Trump (Park Forest, Ill.: Prairie School Press, 1967) and the other with an introduction by William Morgan (New York: Dover, 1969). This book was commissioned by Richardson's neighbors and friends, Charles Sprague Sargent and Frederick Law Olmsted. Van Rensselaer, a contemporary critic, provided an account of Richardson's life and work, with background on his education, approach to design, and office operations. The coverage of Richardson's built work was relatively complete, but the only unbuilt project discussed was the Albany Cathedral (a few others are illustrated in sketches). This book has remained the indispensable beginning for all subsequent research on Richardson. Most copies of the original edition probably remained in the Northeast, although one copy found its way to the offices of Adler and Sullivan in Chicago.

For background on Van Rensselaer, see Cynthia D. Kinnard, "The Life and Works of Mariana Griswold Van Rensselaer, American Art Critic" (Ph.D. diss., Johns Hopkins University, 1977), especially 135–174.

21. *American Architect and Building News* carried seventeen images of Richardson's works between January 1876 and April 1886, the month of his death. In addition, the Albany Cathedral competition drawings were published in September 1883. Between May 1886 and October 1895, twenty-six additional images of Richardson buildings were

published. Richardson's major buildings were documented in a series of small sketches in September 1886, with additional sketches of railroad stations in February 1887. Two photographs of the New York State Capitol appeared in 1898, but these were not identified with Richardson.

22. Photographs of the libraries were published in the following order: North Easton: *American Architect and Building News* 13 (30 June 1883); Quincy: *American Architect and Building News* 13 (30 June 1883); Malden: *American Architect and Building News* 18 (3 October 1885); Woburn: *American Architect and Building News* 19 (1 May 1886); Malden: *American Architect and Building News* 20 (6 November 1886), 24 (22 September 1888).

23. Drawings of the Woburn library design did appear in *American Architect and Building News* 2 (3 March 1877); a drawing of the North Easton library also appeared in *American Architect and Building News* 2 (3 November 1877). This sequence of publication might have indicated the sequence of design to long-term subscribers. However, in its initial years, *American Architect and Building News* was probably not as widely distributed as it was after 1880. Therefore, these early drawings would have been unknown to many later readers, particularly those outside the East.

24. Between early 1885 and late 1886, photographs appeared as follows: Austin Hall, Harvard: *American Architect and Building News* 17 (28 March 1885); Ames Gate Lodge, North Easton: *American Architect and Building News* 18 (26 December 1885); Winn Library, Woburn: *American Architect and Building News* 19 (1 May 1886); Ames Store, Bedford Street, Boston: *American Architect and Building News* 20 (11 September 1886).

25. The Albany City Hall was published in *American Architect and Building News* 26 (13 July 1889); a photograph of the entrance appeared in *American Architect and Building News* 25 (2 March 1889). In addition to the published drawings of the Cincinnati Chamber of Commerce (see note 18), a photograph of the column capitals appeared in *American Architect and Building News* 27 (1 March 1890): 141. The interior was shown in *American Architect and Building News* 29 (12 July 1890): 29.

Images of the Allegheny County Buildings were published in *American Architect and Building News* 28 (24 May 1890); 38 (12 November 1892) and (19 November 1892); and 41 (5 August 1893).

26. Publication of Richardson's masonry houses included Sard: *American Architect and Building News* 24 (1 June 1889); Warder: *American Architect and Building News* 33 (1 August 1891); MacVeagh: *American Architect and Building News* 36 (15 April 1893).

27. A photograph of the Sherman house (1874–1876) in Newport appeared in *American Architect and Building News* 22 (22 October 1887). For clarification of the responsibility for the design, see Jeffrey Karl Ochsner and Thomas C. Hubka, "H. H. Richardson: The Design of the William Watts Sherman House," *Journal of the Society of Architectural Historians* 51 (June 1992): 121–145.

28. Three folios in the series focused on Richardson's buildings: H. H. Richardson, *Austin Hall, Harvard Law School, Cambridge, Mass.,* Monographs of American Architecture 1 (Boston: Ticknor, 1886); H. H. Richardson, *The Ames Memorial Buildings, North Easton, Mass.,* Monographs of American Architecture 3 (Boston: Ticknor, 1886); H. H. Richardson, *Trinity Church, Boston,* Monographs of American Architecture 5 (Boston: Ticknor, 1888). Published separately was H. H. Richardson, *The Billings Library: The Gift to the University of Vermont of Frederick Billings* (Boston: Ticknor, [ca. 1888]).

29. *Inland Architect* published a "Photogravure Edition" beginning in 1887, allowing subscribers who paid more to receive photographic plates in addition to the less expensive line drawings. Photographic images of Richardson's building were published as follows: Adams house, 9 (June 1887); MacVeagh house (two images), 10 (November 1887), and 11 (May 1888); Glessner house, 11 (February 1888); Warder house (two images), 11 (March 1888); J. R. Lionberger house, 11 (June 1888); Marshall Field Wholesale Store, 12 (October 1888); Allegheny County Courthouse (ten images), 13 (May and June 1889); Cincinnati Chamber of Commerce (four images), 12 (January 1889); Gratwick house, 14 (December 1889). In addition, *Inland Architect* carried a series titled "Boston Sketches" in 1888–1889 that included drawings of Richardson's Brattle Square and Trinity Churches (December 1888)

and the Harrison Avenue Ames Building, or J. H. Pray Store (January 1889).

30. Van Rensselaer's 1888 biography, *Henry Hobson Richardson and His Works*, focuses only on Richardson and does not address the context of the time in any detail. It was the first such biography of any American architect. Thus, Richardson was separated from his context at a very early date. My own catalogue raisonné of Richardson's buildings, *H. H. Richardson: Complete Architectural Works,* also sets him apart from the context of his time; however, the catalogue does present his entire known production as an architect, not just his best work.

31. *American Architect and Building News* appeared weekly through the year. The number of plates (drawings and photographs) per issue was usually no more than four, although the number was smaller in the early years and increased thereafter. In 1885 and 1886, *American Architect* launched the Imperial edition, which included additional photographic plates (for an increased price, a subscriber would receive additional photographs of built works). This edition further increased the number of published images, although all subscribers no longer received all images. Richardson, represented by fewer than forty-five plates in the period, may well have had even less than 1.2 percent of all published images.

Richardson's work may have had greater impact than this number suggests, however, because his buildings were published almost exclusively in photographs, whereas most images carried in architectural periodicals at the time were line drawings. In April 1887, after Richardson's death, *American Architect* published a line drawing of Richardson's unbuilt Young Men's Association Library project for Buffalo. This drawing was accompanied by an explanation indicating that during his lifetime, Richardson had not wanted drawings of his unbuilt work published because he thought he could improve it during construction. See *American Architect and Building News* 21 (23 April 1887), text on 199.

32. The Trinity Church tower appeared in *American Architect and Building News* 22 (31 December 1887). Hitchcock did present an interpretation of Richardson in Victorian terms thirty years after the pub-

lication of *Richardson and His Times.* However, it was cast only within Richardson's early career, ending at Trinity Church. See Henry-Russell Hitchcock, *Richardson as a Victorian Architect* (Baltimore: published by Smith College at Barton-Gillette, 1966).

33. Richardson prepared descriptive materials for some competition entries including the Connecticut State Capitol, Hartford; Allegheny County Buildings, Pittsburgh; Chamber of Commerce, Cincinnati; and Hoyt Public Library, East Saginaw, Mich. He also contributed a description for the dedication of Trinity Church. For a complete chronological bibliography, see O'Gorman, *Richardson: Architectural Forms*, 143–159.

34. The use of the term *project* here is derived from its use in psychology and psychoanalysis; to project is "to externalize (a thought or feeling) unconsciously so that it appears to have objective reality" (*Webster's New Universal Dictionary,* 2nd ed., s.v.). Through the process of projection, it is possible for a contemporary architect to have seen a Richardson building in a particular way not necessarily inherent in the design—through a framework projected on the building. The projection is understood to be unconscious, not deliberately chosen. Indeed, Richardson's work might also be considered receptive to projections by architectural historians. Since Richardson did not frame the work for us, we provide the framework. For example, Hitchcock may have interpreted Richardson as a proto-modernist because he saw Richardson through a modern framework that he had (unconsciously) projected, which highlighted the buildings' modern features.

35. Elmer Fisher is quoted in the *Seattle Post-Intelligencer*, 19 October 1889, 5.

36. The Minneapolis-based *Northwestern Architect* published drawings of three of Fisher's Seattle projects: Burke Building (1889–1891), 8 (June 1890); Sullivan Building (1889–1891), 8 (September 1890); Homer Hill Building project (1890), 8 (August 1890).

For general background on Fisher, see Jeffrey Karl Ochsner and Dennis A. Andersen, "Elmer H. Fisher," in *Shaping Seattle Architecture: A Historical Guide to the Architects,* ed. Jeffrey Karl Ochsner (Seattle: University of Washington Press, 1994), 22–27.

37. Hitchcock, *Richardson and His Times*, 262–263. In the revised edition, Hitchcock added lengthy endnotes to bring the book up to date, where he corrected his error of attribution (327 n. XIII-24).

38. Faxon's world was that of Boston in the 1870s and 1880s, where the Ruskinian Gothic of Ware and Van Brunt's Memorial Hall at Harvard and the picturesque Queen Anne were widely admired.

39. For Faxon's Newton Centre church, see *Inland Architect* 13 (April 1889). This image is also found in a volume of plates compiled from several American architectural journals, "American Buildings: Selections," vol. 3, pl. 26; Avery Architectural and Fine Arts Library, Columbia University, New York.

40. The Cambridge City Hall design was published in a drawing in *American Architect and Building News* 24 (28 July 1888).

41. On Longfellow's background and the origins of the firm Longfellow, Alden and Harlow, see Floyd, *Architecture after Richardson*, 21–64. On Richardson's work in relationship to academic eclecticism, see Richard Longstreth, "Academic Eclecticism in American Architecture," *Winterthur Portfolio* 17 (spring 1982): 55–82. A shorter version of this essay is found in Richard Longstreth, *On the Edge of the World: Four Architects in San Francisco at the Turn of the Century* (New York: Architectural History Foundation; Cambridge, Mass.: MIT Press, 1983), 9–39.

42. O'Gorman's division of *H. H. Richardson: Architectural Forms for an American Society* into thematic chapters (titles include "Ruralism," "Urbanism," and "Commuterism") is one indication of the significance of Richardson's designs in offering solutions for particular building types.

43. For publication of Richardson's Ames Store, Bedford Street, Boston, see *American Architect and Building News* 16 (23 August 1884) and (30 August 1884); *American Architect and Building News* 20 (11 September 1886). For his Ames Store, Harrison Avenue, Boston (also called the J. H. Pray and Sons Store), see *American American Architect and Building News* 21 (14 May 1887). For publication of the Marshall Field Wholesale Store, see note 29.

44. A drawing of the Lionberger Wholesale Warehouse appeared in *American Architect and Building News* 21 (21 May 1887); a photograph appeared in *Architectural Record* 1 (October–December 1891): 185. A drawing of the Ames Building, Boston, by Shepley, Rutan and Coolidge appeared in *American Architect and Building News* 26 (13 July 1889) and in *Architectural Record* 1 (October–December 1891): 187.

45. A drawing of the National Bank of Commerce appeared in the supplement to *Northwest Builder, Decorator and Furnisher* 1 (November 1887). The completed building was described and illustrated in several photographs in *Northwestern Architect* 7 (May 1889). Architectural critic Montgomery Schuyler commented favorably on the building: see "Glimpses of Western Architecture: Minneapolis and St. Paul," *Harper's Monthly* 83 (October 1891): 736–755 (reprinted in *American Architecture,* ed. William H. Jordy and Ralph Coe [Cambridge, Mass.: Belknap Press of Harvard University Press, 1961], 292–328).

Harry Wild Jones (1859–1935), originally from Minnesota, was a student in the architecture program at MIT from 1880 to 1882 and is reported to have worked in Richardson's office in 1883. For a partial biographical summary, see Donald R. Torbert, "Minneapolis Architecture and Architects, 1848–1908: A Study of Style Trends in Architecture in a Midwestern City together with a Catalogue of Representative Buildings" (Ph.D. diss., University of Minnesota, 1953), 448–449; on the National Bank of Commerce, see 279–280.

46. A drawing of the New York Times Building, New York, appeared in *Architectural Record* 1 (July–September 1891): 33. A plate is in "American Buildings: Selections," vol. 4, pl. 35, Avery Library, Columbia University. A drawing of the Union Trust Company Building appeared in *Architectural Record* 1 (July–September 1891): 35; *American Architect and Building News* 42 (21 October 1893). On Post's Romanesque Revival commercial buildings, see Winston Weisman, "The Commercial Architecture of George B. Post," *Journal of the Society of Architectural Historians* 31 (October 1972): 176–203.

47. A drawing of the Seattle National Bank Building, Seattle, appeared in *American Architect and Building News* 28 (5 July 1890); a photograph of the corner entrance appeared in *Inland Architect* 23

(March 1894). William Boone's work was never published in an architectural journal. For William Boone and John Parkinson, see Jeffrey Karl Ochsner, "William E. Boone" and "John Parkinson," both in Ochsner, *Shaping Seattle Architecture*, 16–21, 28–33.

48. Long and Kees's competitive design for the Minneapolis Municipal Building and Hennepin County Courthouse appeared in *American Architect and Building News* 23 (7 April 1888); the firm's revised design appeared in *Northwestern Architect* 6 (August 1888).

49. A watercolor of the Pierce County Courthouse appeared in *Northwestern Architect* 8 (October 1890); a photograph of the Los Angeles County Courthouse appeared in *Architectural Record* 1 (July–September 1891): 56. Drawings of two Texas county courthouses by James Riely Gordon and D. E. Laub were published: Victoria County Courthouse (1891–1892) in Victoria, *American Architect and Building News* 54 (17 October 1896); Bexar County Courthouse (1892–1895) in San Antonio, *American Architect and Building News* 46 (20 October 1894).

For an overview of courthouses by Gordon (1863–1937), see Kenneth Breisch, "The Richardsonian Interlude in Texas: A Quest for Meaning and Order at the End of the Nineteenth Century," in *The Spirit of H. H. Richardson on the Midland Prairies: Regional Transformations of an Architectural Style,* ed. Paul C. Larson with Susan M. Brown (Minneapolis: University Art Museum, University of Minnesota; Ames: Iowa State University Press, 1988), 89–101; and Jay C. Henry, "The Richardsonian Romanesque in Texas: An Interpretation," *Texas Architect* 31 (March–April 1981): 53–55. See also Paul Goeldner, "Central Symbols: Historic Texas Courthouses," *Texas Architect* 36 (May–June 1986): 78–85. Examples of Richardsonian courthouses by Gordon and others are illustrated and discussed in Henry-Russell Hitchcock, "Notes on the Architecture," in *Courthouse: A Photographic Document,* ed. Richard Pare (New York: Horizon Press, 1978), 208–224.

50. A drawing of the U.S. Post Office and Courthouse, San Antonio, was published in *American Architect and Building News* 22 (13 August 1887). For the Office of the Supervising Architect, see Lois A. Craig

and the Staff of the Federal Architecture Project, *The Federal Presence: Architecture, Politics, and National Design* (Cambridge, Mass.: MIT Press, 1984), 162–169; and Bates Lowry, *Building a National Image: Architectural Drawings for the American Democracy, 1879–1912* (Washington, D.C.: National Building Museum, 1985), 58–88.

51. Published illustrations of Richardsonian library designs include Richmond Memorial Library, Richmond, Vt., by James G. Cutler, in *American Architect and Building News* 24 (22 September 1888); Memorial Library, Lexington, Ky., by Willis Polk, in *American Architect and Building News* 25 (9 March 1889); Acton Memorial Library (1889), Acton, Mass., by Hartwell and Richardson, in *American Architect and Building News* 25 (29 June 1889); New London Library (1889–1890), New London, Conn., by Shepley, Rutan and Coolidge in *American Architect and Building News* 33 (26 September 1891) and in *Architectural Record* 1 (October–December 1891): 178.

A photograph of the Rindge Public Library, Cambridge, Mass. (1887–1889), by Van Brunt and Howe, appeared in *Inland Architect* 16 (January 1890) and *American Architect and Building News* 36 (11 June 1892), and was included in "American Buildings: Selections," vol. 2, pl. 99, Avery Library, Columbia University.

For a general discussion of Richardson's libraries and their influence, see Kenneth A. Breisch, *Henry Hobson Richardson and the Small Public Library in America: A Study in Typology* (Cambridge, Mass.: MIT Press, 1997).

52. Stations by Richardson and by Shepley, Rutan and Coolidge for the Boston and Albany Railroad are addressed as a coherent group in Jeffrey Karl Ochsner, "Architecture for the Boston and Albany Railroad, 1881–1894," *Journal of the Society of Architectural Historians* 47 (June 1988): 109–131. Even Hitchcock characterized the Boston and Albany Station at Allston by Shepley, Rutan and Coolidge as "particularly fine" (*Richardson and His Times*, 224n).

A drawing of Shepley, Rutan and Coolidge's Boston and Albany Station at Springfield appeared in *American Architect and Building News* 23 (31 March 1888); images of the constructed building were published in *Architectural Record* 1 (October–December 1891): 189, 191. Published drawings of Richardsonian railroad stations by other architects included those by Van Brunt and Howe for the Union Pacific and the Central Pacific railroads: Ogden, Utah, in *American Architect and Building News* 20 (6 November 1886); and Cheyenne, Wyo., in *American Architect and Building News* 21 (8 January 1887).

53. Arthur Vinal's Boston Water Works, Chestnut Hill, appeared in *Northwestern Architect* 7 (February 1889); these images are also found in "American Buildings: Selections," vol. 2, pls. 110–111, Avery Library, Columbia University. O'Gorman characterizes Vinal's design as "picturesque Romanesque" (*Richardson: Architectural Forms*, 67–68).

54. Romanesque revival masonry houses can be found, for example, on Summit Avenue in St. Paul and on private streets in St. Louis. For St. Paul, see Ernest R. Sandeen, *St. Paul's Historic Summit Avenue* (St. Paul: Macalester College Museum, 1978). For St. Louis, see Charles C. Savage, *Architecture of the Private Streets of St. Louis: The Architects and the Houses They Designed* (Columbia: University of Missouri Press, 1987), and Julius K. Hunter, *Westmoreland and Portland Places: The History and Architecture of America's Premier Private Streets,* 1888–1988 (Columbia: University of Missouri Press, 1988).

Margaret Henderson Floyd was Professor of Art and Architectural History at Tufts University.

Thomas C. Hubka is Professor of Architecture at the University of Wisconsin-Milwaukee.

Francis R. Kowsky is Professor of Art History at Buffalo State College.

Maureen Meister is Associate Professor of Art History at the Art Institute of Boston.

Jeffrey Karl Ochsner, FAIA, is Professor of Architecture at the University of Washington.

James F. O'Gorman is Grace Slack McNeil Professor of the History of American Art at Wellesley College.

William H. Pierson, Jr., is Massachusetts Professor of Art Emeritus at Williams College

Index of Names